Vincent Ball was b
Wales, on the 4th o
of becoming a 'cow   ......s took him
on an adventure that included serving in the
RAAF in World War Two, working his way to
England on a tramp steamer and winning a
scholarship to The Royal Academy of Dramatic
Art, London. He worked as an actor in England
for 25 years—waiting to be discovered and
whisked off to Hollywood! He returned to
Australia in 1973.

Vincent Ball has been married to Doreen for 47
years. They have three children and one
grandchild.

BUCK JONES,
WHERE ARE YOU?

AN AUSTRALIAN BOY'S ADVENTURE

VINCENT
BALL

RANDOM HOUSE
A U S T R A L I A

Random House Australia Pty Ltd
20 Alfred Street, Milsons Point, NSW 2061

Sydney   New York   Toronto
London   Auckland   Johannesburg
and agencies throughout the world

First published 1996
Copyright © Vincent Ball, 1996.

National Library of Australia
Cataloguing-in-Publication Data

Ball, Vincent, 1923– .
Buck Jones where are you?

ISBN 0 09 183262 4

1. Ball, Vincent, 1923– . 2. Actors – Australia –
Biography. I. Title.

792.8092
Designed by Yolande Gray
Typeset by Midland Typesetters, Maryborough, Victoria
Printed by Griffin Paperbacks, Adelaide

Dedicated to
Buck Jones, Tom Mix and Tim McCoy
who, when I was a boy, made me
want to ride tall in the saddle.

FOREWORD

WHEN VINCE FIRST told me that he'd written a book which was actually to be published, my heart sank just a little. I knew I'd be expected to read it and perhaps even buy it, and my experience of most actors' autobiographies had left me more than a little jaundiced. I wasn't looking forward to yet another account of 'what I told Sir Peter Hall' or what 'David Lean said to me'. As a fellow actor I've had the odd suggestion made that my own autobiography might be worth a read and I've always replied that I had nothing significant or particularly interesting to say about anything or anyone that wouldn't be either anachronistic or libellous and probably both. As far as I was concerned, the 'Actor's Autobiography' started and stopped with *The Moon is a Balloon*, and

David Niven I most certainly am not. Neither, I thought, much as I love him, is Vince.

We first met in the Libyan desert in 1958 when we were making a film together and have been firm friends ever since. Over the intervening thirty-seven years we've shared innumerable jolly days and nights of golf and snooker and poker and cricket and general boozing and laughter, but literature and serious writing were topics which seldom engaged our attention. I have written the occasional script and Peter Yeldham, a great mutual friend, is a serious 'proper' writer, quite rightly held in some awe by the likes of Vince and myself; but apart from the usual actor's condemnation of the quality of the scripts and writers we may have to work with, the world of literature was fairly peripheral to our lives. Or so I thought.

About a year ago in Wyong, a long long way from Libya, Vince gave me his manuscript, hesitantly and modestly I hasten to add, and I, without showing the reluctance and trepidation I did my best to hide, took the manuscript away and read it.

Oh joy ... oh rapture! Not an actor's reminiscences at all. A few references of course to the world of showbiz and his place in it, and contribution to it, but no 'sharing a joke with Larry', no semi-indiscreet revelation of how 'I won the heart and loins of X,Y, or Z'. This is a wonderful story of how a kid from the outback grew up and went to war and coped with peace and life in England and Australia and grew into the mature and lovely old codger he is today.

It is part *Candide*, part *A Fortunate Life*, but mostly Vincent Ball telling a story which is engaging, funny, thoughtful and above all a smashing read.

Michael Craig.

CONTENTS

ACKNOWLEDGMENTS

THIS BOOK WOULD never have seen the light of day if it hadn't been for the help and encouragement of my dear wife Doreen, and Anthony Wheeler; the advice and suggestions of Peter and Marge Yeldham, and my friendly proofreaders John and Janet Croyston. Eric and Lyn Tayler read and re-read the manuscript as it slowly neared completion and for their comments and encouragement I shall always be grateful. To mates Bill Kerr, Michael Craig, Leo McKern, Brenda Ennis, Brenda Houston and Oliver Waring, thank you for taking time out to read it.

Dear friends, your 'Why don't you try and get it published?' gave me the incentive to send what I wrote to Random House, where Julia Stiles had the courage with a capital 'C' to do just that and Bernadette Foley, editor extraordinary, helped me with me gramma.

Now on with the motley.

PROLOGUE

'I'VE BEEN TELLING you for years,' Doreen said. 'You should leave Nicky and our future grandchildren a record of your life as an actor. It only needs to be a thumbnail sketch. When you're on the beach, instead of concentrating on the topless young ladies, concentrate on your memoirs. It's better for your blood pressure.'

'Very funny,' I said. 'Anyway, there's a tin trunk full of stuff about my life and career under the house.'

'Nobody's going to wade through that lot,' she so rightly replied.

'What? Tell them that I did this, and then I did that, and then I did this, and then ... they won't know who or what I'm talking about and they probably couldn't care less. I'd bore the pants off them. I can't see them being excited by the fact that I did *A Town Like Alice* in 1954 when they're living in the twenty-first century.'

'Try,' said Doreen. 'Just try. It'll keep you occupied. You can add it to that writing you did about twenty years ago, when you were touring in England. Remember?'

'That writing' was to keep me out of the pub at lunchtime while I was on tour. Bradford, Leeds and Manchester in winter can be pretty dreary during the day and that lunchtime drink was a bit of a trap. I couldn't handle it and be at my best for the evening performance. Doreen had suggested that I write five hundred words a day, to keep me out of the pub and to exercise my brain while sitting in front of the gas fire in various digs, in various northern cities, waiting to go to the theatre.

I'm no novelist, no creator of fiction, all I could write about was something I knew well: 'Me'. So what started out as an exercise finished up as a bit of an ego trip, a potted history of my life 'pre' actor.

Now, twenty years later, I'm supposed to find those notebooks, put them into some sort of order and add a 'thumbnail sketch' of my career as an actor so you, my dear grandchildren, can read all about me in years to come.

I can hear your parents saying it now, 'If you don't smarten up and behave yourself, I'll make you read your grandpa's memoirs again.'

And the reply: 'Oh no. *Not* the memoirs. *Anything* but the memoirs!'

So here I am in the year 1995, a 71-year-old, grey-haired actor sitting on the island at Balmoral Beach, Sydney, Australia, watching the sailing boats manoeuvring their way around the harbour and a few sailboard riders weaving in and out between them, showing-off their skills to the many topless young ladies reclining on the beach, when I should be writing my memoirs; turning my forty years as an actor into a 'thumbnail sketch' for all my unborn grandchildren.

Buck Jones, Tom Mix and Tim McCoy, you were my boyhood heroes. All I wanted, was to be like you—a cowboy on the films.

One

DAYDREAMING

'COME ON, BROWNIE.'

The only answer I got from our jersey cow was the flick of her tail as she brushed off the flies; left side, right side, left side, right side, left, right. Gee, it was hot; the heat sort of made waves that spread across the hard road as me, Brownie and Bindy, my kangaroo dog, made our way home.

Bindy was a beautiful brindle bitch. One day I was gunna enter her for the maiden stakes at the new greyhound racetrack they had opened at the showground. Dad said I'd have to train her properly and give her good food, like rabbit, not scraps all the time, and rub her down and not bring her home tired every day, like she was now, head hanging low, tongue lolling out the side of her mouth.

Serves Bindy right. Every afternoon she tries

to catch all the rabbits around Moree, and around Moree there are millions and millions of rabbits. You'd swear that the whole plains were moving; they looked like a huge grey carpet speckled with white dots. I suppose to Bindy, in her doggy world, the rabbits looked like a lot of dinners running around. She'd start off by catching a couple when she was fresh but as the afternoon wore on she'd be so tired the rabbits would be running circles around her. Still, she'd catch a couple. Maybe she knew that if she didn't she'd have to eat scraps.

We lived in a small wooden house on an acre and a half on the corner of Auburn Street. It was like a lot of other houses around Moree: iron roof, bull-nosed verandah, four rooms with the kitchen, laundry and bathroom connected to the main house by a covered passageway. The dunny was right down near the back fence and the windmill and the well, where all the snakes lived, were between the house and the dunny.

Hardly anybody ever went to the dunny at night!

It was a real good home with a beaut big yard with a cow shed, chook yard, fruit trees and a vegetable patch. There was always something

to do and the Ball kids did all the doing.

Brian, me, Clete and Joe slept on the front verandah; Mum and Dad in one of the front rooms; and Moya and Noni in a back room. The other front room was the sitting room and there was a gramophone, two armchairs and a sofa in it, but nobody ever sat in the sitting room! The other back room was empty and was called the 'lumber room'. I don't know why it was called that, it was just the 'lumber room'. The kitchen was big with a large stove that kept me and Brian busy chopping wood to keep it going. It was the best room in the house, warm, cosy, and always smelling of Mum's cooking. Yeah, it was a real good home.

Flick left, flick right, get up every morning, serve Mass, milk Brownie. Some days she was easy to find, she'd stay near the town. Other days she'd take it into her head to explore the whole Australian bush and I reckon I'd walk about six miles before I'd find her. It was a six-mile day today, but she didn't seem to care. She seemed to know that she helped to make the Ball family one of the healthiest around; milk, milk, it was everywhere. Mum would boil it so as it would keep, dishes of it with thick skin

cream on top you could wind round your finger. Rice pudding, junket, bread pudding, milk . . . milk.

When I got home I'd do the milking, cut some grass for Brownie at Mrs Wild's, feed the dogs. I dunno, I was always feeding something, cow, chooks, dogs. I must get Dad to mend my boots, there are two big nails right through the soles. It was a lot less painful to take your chances with the bindi-eyes and cats-eyes and not wear them. At the moment they were slung over my shoulders with the two rabbits Bindy had caught.

'G'day, Snow.'

'G'day, Mr McCauley.'

'Bit late bringin' Brownie home, aren't yer?'

'I couldn't find her, she was over behind the power station with the hospital cows.'

Mr McCauley wiped the sweat off his big, red, round face and leaned on the fork he'd been digging with. Golly, he was fat. Dad reckoned he was eighteen stone. He was always working near the fence so that he could have a yarn with everyone who passed. But all the people in Moree were a wake-up to him and nobody ever stopped, because if you did you could never get

away. He was there every afternoon when I came by, and it always started off the same.

'G'day, Snow.'

'G'day, Mr McCauley.' And then it would be—

'How's yer dad, Snow?'

'Oh fine, Mr McCauley.'

'I hear your brother Brian's a pretty good tennis player.'

'Yeah, he's real good, Mr McCauley.'

He always asked a different question every day. I suppose I'd miss him if he wasn't there of an afternoon.

Brian was the eldest, he was about sixteen months older than me. Then there was Moya and Noni and then Cletus and Joe.

Brian was a good big brother, a real hard worker and always willing to do more than his share. Between the two of us, we looked after Brownie and the milking, cut grass, fed the chooks, chopped wood, collected the eggs, killed the odd chook for Easter and Christmas, and that job which we didn't like at all—washing up after tea at night. We couldn't wait for Moya and Noni to grow up so they could take over.

Whenever I met anybody, they'd say, 'G'day, Snow. How's Brian?'

Everybody liked him.

The flies were worse than ever now, they kept circling Brownie's rump as she flicked her tail. I could feel a trickle of sweat running down my back and the rabbits seemed to be growing heavier. I'd just like to be swimming out at the 'Three Mile' right now, letting the cool water rush over me, then I'd sit on the bank and eat some of those wild watermelons that grow in one of the little gullies.

Still it's Saturday tomorrow. Do Mrs Spicer's messages—threepence—clear the backyard, chop some wood—threepence—and I had ninepence in my moneybox—one and threepence. Sixpence for the pictures and ninepence for the hot pie and gravy and peas at the Greek cafe. Hope Mum has lunch ready early so I won't be late for the pictures, don't want to miss any of it. Wouldn't anyway because I'd rather miss my lunch. A special double feature, Tim McCoy in the first and Buck Jones in the second, two of my favourite cowboys. It would be worth saving up for. I hadn't been to the pictures for three

weeks and I'd missed some of my other favourites, Tom Mix, Ken Maynard and Hoot Gibson.

Gee, wouldn't it be great to be a cowboy in
the films? Two six-guns slung low and tied with
a leather thong around your legs—the mark of
a gunslinger—cowboy boots, big Stetson, chaps,
kerchief, lariat, and a beautiful white stallion,
just like Silver, Buck Jones's horse.

The slow walk down the main street at sun-
up, spurs jingling, the sun glinting on my sheriff's badge, a lazy crooked smile lurking around
my mouth as I move forwards towards the killer
who had called me out in front of the whole
town; a town that now peered at us from behind
closed windows and doors. I could see the killer's cruel face, the small puffs of dust as he
moved slowly forward, hands poised like claws
above his guns . . .

My cold, steely blue eyes narrowed as I
slowly tied my boots to Brownie's tail. I needed
room to move but I always gave a man more
than a fair chance. I let them draw first. There'd
been plenty of showdowns over the years, since
I'd got the name of 'the fastest gun in the West',
but there was always some killer who thought
he was faster.

The gap between the two of us was growing smaller, I could hear the jingle of his spurs as Big Jake McCready moved towards me with a catlike tread. Not a sound could be heard as the whole town waited . . .

Big Jake was just about to draw when Brownie let out a bellow and took off. But instead of taking the back way home, she decided that the main street of Moree was a good place to show-off. So one crazed jersey cow with a pair of boots tied to her tail, a blond, ten-year-old boy carrying a couple of dead rabbits, and a tired kangaroo dog, startled the whole town. Brownie was bellowing, Bindy was barking and being helped by every other dog in the town. Cries of 'Good on yer, Snow', and wide-eyed women calling their children off the road, then a noise that seemed to be louder than all the others.

'Wait till I get you home!'

My dad!

I saw him out of the corner of my eye as he came out of a side street, on his way home from work.

'Why did yer tie yer boots to Brownie's tail?'

'I dunno, Dad. I must have been daydreamin'.'

'Daydreamin'? Strewth, I've always told yer to bring her home quietly. If she gets excited she won't let her milk down.'

Mum laughed till the tears rolled down her cheeks, ruffled my hair and said, 'Go and finish your work, and give your boots to your father so as he can fix those nails.' By this time, the rest of the family were home, all bursting with different stories of Brownie and the boots.

'Come on, yer silly cow! Let yer milk down.'

I liked daydreaming because then I could be anybody I wanted to be, and if I was working, like cutting grass for Brownie, it somehow made it easier. It was alright daydreaming cutting grass but when you were up a tree cutting branches you had to be pretty careful. I'd fallen a couple of times when I'd made the mistake of going for my gun and letting go of my hold.

I was cutting grass near the Common and I was gunna be Tim McCoy today, when the honk of a horn made me jump. It was Father Tuttle, waving his hand, his old Ford full of priests. They must be the Jesuit missionaries who had

come down from New Guinea. They spent a week at each country town having a spell from working up in the jungle. It was called Mission Week and they were starting on Monday, which meant that I'd have to serve three Masses every morning for the week: six and six-thirty am, miss seven and seven-thirty, then serve eight. I always fell asleep in the vestry while seven and seven-thirty were being said. Sister Mary Ellis would put my head on her lap and wake me up in time for eight.

I liked Sister Mary Ellis, somehow she didn't look like a nun. She was so young and pretty and she sort of skipped about everywhere. Mother Confiteor was always telling her to walk and not run and Father Tuttle was always pulling her leg and making her laugh and when she laughed you had to sort of laugh with her, you just couldn't help it. But she could be real strict. She had to give me the cane once. I'd been caught smoking behind the tennis shed. Well, I hadn't really been caught. I'd chewed pepper leaves to take away the smell and then had been sick over my desk. Somehow she knew that I'd been smoking and we'd been warned that if we were caught we'd get the cane on

each hand. She said that being sick was enough punishment but she had to stick to her promise and give me the cane.

I went out to the front of the class and Sister Mary Ellis got the cane and tested it, bending it backward and forwards.

'Put out your right hand. This is going to hurt me more than it hurts you,' she said.

That's what Mum always said. I could never understand why they always said that, I was the one who was gunna get beaten. It would hurt me more than it did them.

She looked at me and gave me a bit of a smile and then looked at my hand, which was stretched out very stiff. I stared out the window and kept staring till it was all over. She gave me three on the right, three on the left, three on the right, three on the left. Then she just stood there looking at me for a bit. She had the same kind of look on her face Mum had after she'd given me a hiding. I'll bet if there'd been nobody in the classroom, she would've given me a big hug. She turned quickly away and I went back to my desk. It's funny but I never cried when I got the cane. Well you couldn't very well, not in front of the whole class.

'Will you copy down the sums on the black-board and do them for your homework tonight.'

Strewth. My hands by now were so stiff and swollen I couldn't hold the pencil. I couldn't feel anything. I just sat there trying, but my writing looked like a spider had walked across the page.

Sister Mary Ellis stood by my side watching me for a bit. I wanted so much to copy down those sums, I'd show her, but I just couldn't make that bloody pencil work. She didn't say anything and went back to her desk. A few minutes later, she came back and put a piece of paper in front of me. On it were all the sums copied out. I looked up and said, 'Thank you Sister.' She gave a little smile and walked away.

Funny, but the following morning I'd be an altar boy again, fast asleep in the vestry, using her lap as a pillow.

I'd been made an altar boy when I was six and a half. As soon as I was able to read the nuns taught me to serve Mass. It was all in Latin. I'd learned it like a parrot. I didn't know what the priest was saying and I didn't know what I was saying.

I remember the first Mass that I had to serve on my own, I was so nervous that I dropped the

Missal. That's the big book with all the ribbons in it that the priest reads from. It went bouncing all the way down the steps, with me after it. I lost Father McDermott's place—I'd put the ribbons back in the wrong pages and he didn't know where he was. He was muttering away to himself, looking down at me. It seemed to be ages before he got going again. When we came off he went crook at me. He said the Missal was worth about fifty pounds and I was to be more careful in future. I couldn't help it if I was small. I was only just able to reach the altar by standing on tip-toe.

Next day I was serving Mass for Father Tuttle. Everything was going along fine until I brought him a little bowl of water and a towel to wash and dry his hands. While he was doing it, he seemed to flick his fingers and a spray of water hit me right in the face. Ah, I must be dreaming, priests don't do things like that, not while they're saying Mass. Next morning the same thing happened. Father Tuttle's been flicking water in my face for three years now, it's a part of the secret game we have between ourselves.

Some priests don't drink all the wine out of

the crucible that we bring them during Mass, but Father Tuttle always drank the lot. He'd fill the crucible right to the top before Mass and make sure I poured the whole lot into the chalice. The way he drank it didn't seem to be very holy and he sort of smacked his lips afterwards. The wine must be pretty good, I thought, if Father Tuttle carries on like that, so me and Fatty Picone, another altar boy, decided to have a go at it. One afternoon after school we got into the vestry through the church and then down into the cellar where the wine was kept. There seemed to be hundreds and hundreds of bottles of it. We found a corkscrew, so we opened a bottle. It tasted real nice. No wonder Father Tuttle smacked his lips. We drank the whole bottle.

To begin with we felt real good and sort of funny. Y'know ... sort of ... funny. We were laughing a lot. I think we were both drunk. Fatty and me were as sick as dogs against the big gum tree in our backyard.

I've never tasted altar wine since.

Sunday was a big day for serving Mass; there'd be the sermon, and during the sermon you'd sit on the altar steps and look at the congregation.

It made you feel real important and especially today because it was my first Palm Sunday and I'd be helping to hand out the palms.

I could see Mum and Dad and the rest of the family, Nora Nell and Mick Ellis. Mick wasn't paying any attention at all, he was looking at Nora Nell. Bluey Baker wasn't there, maybe he was going to late Mass. Mick was still looking at Nora but she was paying attention to what the priest was saying and not taking any notice of him. She was real pretty with long fair hair and big blue eyes, and little brown freckles over her nose.

Whenever I was daydreaming and being a cowboy hero like Buck Jones, the girl I was saving always looked like Nora Nell. That bloody Mick is still looking at Nora ... he should be listening to Father English who was going on about the evils of drink and glaring right at a bunch of men at the back of the church. 'The Catholic drinkers of Moree', that's what Bluey called them. They were always late and fell asleep during Mass and the priest spent the whole sermon trying to wake them up.

I had wanted to go to the lavatory just before Mass started but there wasn't enough

time, and I thought I could hang out until it was over. But by now the pain was pretty crook and I didn't know what to do. I couldn't just walk out of Mass when everybody could see me.

Gee, I wish Father English would hurry up with the sermon. He was now telling us all about faith, hope and charity, then there'd be a lot of communion because it was first Mass.

Bloody hell, the pain was pretty awful now.

Towards the end of the Mass I was too frightened to move, I just knelt there. I don't think I've ever prayed so hard in all my life, but I wasn't praying for my soul, I was praying that God would help me. The sisters and priests were always telling me that He was understanding and kind and forgiving and as I was an altar boy, I reckoned He ought to be more understanding than usual.

I started running as soon as we got into the vestry, down the steps and straight across the school playground to the lavatory about a hundred yards away. I was the best runner in Moree for my age and even wearing slippers and my surplice and cassock, I felt I'd never run faster.

About twenty yards from the lavatory it all

happened. I suppose it must have been the running that did it.

I'd been in the lavatory for about two hours before I heard Brian calling.

'Snow?'

'I'm in here.'

'Where?'

'In the dunny.'

'What are you doin' in there? Gee, Snow, what a mess.'

He looked at me for a bit, then burst out laughing. I don't blame him, I was covered in it.

'You wait here, Snow. I'll go home and get some clothes for you.'

'Brian, don't tell anybody.'

It wasn't long before he was back with some clothes and some paper to wrap my dirty things in and a towel to clean up with. By this time I was attracting the flies, but I did the best I could.

'I'll walk on ahead, Snow.'

I know why he said that, because we'd be walking into the wind. I just hoped I didn't meet anybody.

'Let's run, Brian.'

So that's how we went home, Brian about twenty yards ahead of me.

'Faster, Brian.'

Brian somehow knew when I was getting near him because he would put a spurt on, maybe he could smell me.

Mum didn't mind the smell. She took me into the laundry where there was a big tub of hot water, took off my clothes and scrubbed me real clean. Then she made me feel a real sis, she put Johnson's Baby Powder all over me. Brian reckoned I still smelt, only this time like a sheila.

Brian was pretty good, he never did tell anybody.

I suppose that was my worst day of being an altar boy.

The best days, of course, were when there was a funeral. I know it wasn't very good for the person who had died or for their families and friends, but for me it meant that I got out of school to toll the bell and maybe go to the cemetery. Tolling the bell was the best part of it because you had to climb right up to the top of the bell tower and, as Father Tuttle said, you had to make the bell sound sad and mournful. This meant that you'd hit the bell with the clapper just once, and as the sound was dying away, you'd hit it again. I dunno, but it made you feel

very important because everybody could hear it all over Moree and they'd know another Catholic was dead.

Sometimes I knew the person who had died and the slow *dong ... dong ... dong* of the bell would bring me out in goose pimples. I felt that I was sort of offering up a prayer of music and it would help them get into Heaven by cutting down their stay in Purgatory.

Father English said that very few people were pure enough to go straight to Heaven, they had to spend a bit of time in Purgatory. That's why we were always praying for somebody or having a Mass said for them. But you never knew when to stop because you never knew when they got out of Purgatory, so you just kept on praying. I hoped that if they had gone to Heaven and didn't need your prayers any more, that the prayers went to somebody else to give them a bit of a hand.

I didn't go to all the funerals because the sisters reckoned I was too young. They said it wasn't good for me to see all those sad people, a lot would be crying and sometimes one of them wouldn't want to leave the grave, even when they started shovelling dirt onto the coffin, and

they would have to be dragged away screaming and yelling.

Everybody was supposed to be sad at funerals but sometimes I'd sort of look around, just moving my eyes, pretending I was looking down, and I reckon that some of them didn't look as sad as they ought to. I swear that one bloke was smiling, or if he wasn't, it was a funny way to cry.

'Hey Snow, yer ever wagged school?'

'No Bluey.'

'Well, why don't yer give it a go tomorrow?'

'What about me mum and dad? Me dad'd kill me if he found out.'

'You'll be home at the same time. They'll never know. We could go out to the "Three Mile" swimmin'. We'll take our shanghais. Are yer game?'

'But Bluey, when yer miss school you've got to take a note.'

'Yer tell 'em yer were sick and you'll bring the note the next day, but yer never do and then they forget about it. Now are yer game?'

'Yeah, I'm game.'

'I'll meet yer at the old slaughterhouse about eight. Okay?'

'Okay.'

But I wasn't really game. I just wanted Bluey to think that I was. It was all a bit scary, just thinking about it, you know, like when you're stealing fruit. Anyway, I don't think wagging school's a sin. I know stealing is because it's one of the Ten Commandments, 'Thou shalt not steal'. There's no 'Thou shalt not wag school'. It's all the lies that you have to tell that are the sins.

Cripes. I'm already worrying about whether wagging school is a sin or not. It would just be nice sometimes to do things and not have to think if they're a sin. Everything I did seemed to be a toss-up between Heaven, Hell and Purgatory. At least, being baptised, I didn't have to worry about Limbo.

Swimming at the Three Mile next day wasn't much fun. All I could think about was what I was going to tell Sister Mary Ellis and what if Mum and Dad found out and would I go home first and dump my school bag like I always did and then look for Brownie, or what. So far wagging school was a lousy way to spend a day. Bluey said I was like a 'great big sheila' the way I was going on. 'Stop worryin' Snow, yer drivin' me crazy.'

Worrying? Maybe Bluey's dad wasn't as strict as mine.

We swam for quite a bit, then sat on the river bank and ate our sandwiches, swapping soggy tomato for soggy beetroot. We didn't really do much ... a bit of bird-nesting, looked around for some snakes, chased a few rabbits. But we didn't try to kill any of them, because we couldn't take them home anyway ... we were supposed to be at school.

I found Brownie over near the hospital and by the time I got home it was about five o'clock.

Mum was at the back door watching me put Brownie in the bails ready for milking. Maybe it was the way she was standing or maybe it was the way she was looking but I knew she knew that I'd wagged school. I could feel my face going red as I walked towards her. She held out the milk bucket.

'After you've done the milking, you'd better go to the lumber room and wait for your father. Sister Mary Ellis sent Jacky McDermott over to find out if you were sick. She wanted to know if you'd be well enough to serve Mass for the Mission Fathers tomorrow morning.'

Waiting in the lumber room was always the

worst part; wondering what kind of mood Dad would be in and would he hit hard, and would he use his thin belt or his thick belt? I used to be brave, like all the young movie stars who always 'took their beating like a man', and didn't cry. Well, I used to be like that but not any more, because when you didn't cry or make noises Dad often thought he wasn't hurting you and you weren't sorry, so he hit harder. So instead, I would start yelling and crying and saying, 'I'm sorry, Dad. I won't do it again, Dad. I'm sorry, Dad. I'm sorry, Dad, I won't do it again, I promise. I'm sorry, Dad ... I'm sorry, Dad,' at the same time dodging around, trying to protect my legs and bum from his belt.

I used to make so much noise that Mum would sometimes knock on the door and call out, 'Don't overdo it, Alf.'

It always ended up with Dad giving me one of his fierce looks and saying, 'Let that be a lesson to you. Don't do it again.' And then at the door, turning and flipping me a threepenny bit with, 'Don't tell yer mother.'

Sometimes you were lucky and got sixpence. Dad didn't always have the right change. Maybe this time he'd go a bit easy, because I bet he'd

wagged school a few times when he was young. And I bet the reason he often went easy with his belt was because after a hard day's work the last thing he wanted to do was to come home and start belting one of his kids. Knowing Dad, he would just like to sit down, have a nice cup of tea and a pipe.

I'd already made up my mind not to wag school again, it was too much trouble because you spent the whole day worrying about what was gunna happen if Mum and Dad found out— and then there'd be Sister Mary Ellis's cane. A sixer on each hand for wagging school.

The door opened and Dad came in. He didn't say anything, just started to unbuckle his belt. Just my luck, he was wearing his thick one. He moved towards me.

'You wagged school.'

'I'm sorry, Dad ... I'm sorry, Dad ... I won't do it again ... I'm ...'

I handed Sister Mary Ellis the note Mum had given me. She read it, looked at me for a bit, then said, 'Will you stand out in front of the class.'

Cripes, I was hoping that the note would've said that I'd wagged school and had been punished for it. I still had the red marks on my bum

to prove it. Bluey was sitting at his desk. He gave me a bit of a smile and winked.

I took a sixer on each hand.

As I sat down at my desk, nursing my throbbing hands, I whispered to Bluey, 'Did yer get the cane?'

'What for?'

'For waggin' school yesterday.'

Bluey grinned. 'Waggin' school? I was sick yesterday. I'm bringin' a note tomorrow.'

Well at least I'd be able to go to the pictures on Saturday with the sixpence Dad had flipped me as he left the room.

'Wagging school is like lying and cheating,' Mum said the next day. 'You'd better go to confession this Saturday.'

I dunno what the Protestant kids did, but being a Catholic was one long battle to stay out of going to Hell. If you committed a mortal sin, the thing was to get to confession as soon as you could, in case you died and went to Hell for all eternity. But a venial sin got you into Purgatory, which didn't seem to be so bad because you only suffered for a couple of hundred years or until your soul was cleansed and then off you went to

Heaven. I seemed to spend most of my life sinning, confessing, going to communion and even after making an act of perfect contrition and promising never to sin again, I'd weaken and be at it a couple of days later. 'Hell fire and damnation' were the terrible words the priests kept telling us about during religious instruction. I seemed to spend more time in a state of fear than I ever did in a state of grace.

Going to confession was alright if you got Father Tuttle or Father English, but Father McDermott, who used to visit Moree now and then, was very different. He was real strict and would give you a lot of penance and a good talking to before he'd let you go and if you were a long time in the confession box, the people waiting to have their confessions knew you'd committed a lot of sins and they'd all stare at you when you came out. I knew he was in town because I'd seen him driving around in his T-Model Ford.

The church was pretty crowded on Saturday when I got there and I'd have a bit of a wait for my turn. It had been two weeks since my last confession and I dunno, but I seemed to have sinned a lot. I'd wagged school, had

'bad intentions' to tell lies to Mum and Dad about it, had blasphemed four times when I was with Bluey—you know, 'taking Our Lord's name in vain'—had stolen some oranges from Mr O'Neal's backyard and had more bad thoughts. I just hoped Father McDermott wasn't hearing confessions because he always asked, 'Bad thoughts about what?' I seemed to have broken half of the Ten Commandments. Some I didn't understand like 'Thou shalt not commit adultery', but nobody ever told us what that one meant when they were teaching us the catechism, we'd just say it. Anyway, Bluey reckoned you had to be grown up and married to do that one. Also I didn't understand about not doing 'servile works on Sundays', but Bluey, who knew about such things, said that if you were a good Catholic, you just had to sit around and do nothing on that day.

My turn came and in I went. The small door slid back and Father McDermott and I stared at each other. He looked so fierce, and because I'd been thinking about all my sins, I just got up in fright and ran. I heard 'Come back here!' as he took off after me. I went straight down the centre aisle with Father McDermott close

behind, yelling, 'Vincent Ball, come back here, do you hear?' He caught me just as I got down the front steps of the church. The people in church really had something to stare at now as I was led back to the confession box. There was a lot of whispering and shaking of heads.

'Why did you run away?'

'I dunno, Father . . . I was scared . . . I have a lot of sins to confess and . . .'

'Do I frighten you?'

'No . . . er . . . yes. I dunno, Father. I'm sorry.'

'How old are you?'

'Nine, Father.'

'Nine, I see. Alright, let's hear about all of these terrible sins you've committed.'

When I'd finished confessing, he said, 'Is that all?'

'Yes Father.'

He looked at me for a bit, not saying anything. There was just this silence. I'll bet he was working out how big my penance was gunna be.

'For your penance, say two Hail Marys and two Our Fathers. Now say an Act of Perfect Contrition.'

He wasn't so bad after all.

Bluey and me came out of the pictures slowly, in a sort of a crouch, our hands hanging loosely by our sides, ready for a quick draw, just like Buck Jones whom we'd just seen capture the Mountain Raiders, a wild gang of cattle rustlers, single handed. Aw crikey, wouldn't it be good to be like that, real game, always on the side of the law, protecting the ...

'Snow, what about on Saturday we go and raid the "pats" garden? Mick says he's game. We could get some watermelons.'

Bugger, I thought, here we go again.

Every time I said, 'Yeah, I'm game', I ended up in trouble. The word 'game' was the most important word us kids used. It was the way we judged other kids and ourselves.

Are yer game? Yer not game enough. Yeah, yeah, yer not game. He's a game kid. He wouldn't be game enough. He's gamer than you. He's too game. He's a game 'un. And when you're asked, 'Are yer game?' you're not game enough to say no, so you end up being game and getting into trouble, because you don't want anybody to think that you're not game. I just wish that sometimes I was game enough to say 'I'm not game'.

'Yeah, alright, Bluey. I'm game ... we'll take the dogs.'

The 'pats' garden was the name of the Chinese place near the river where they grew fruit and vegetables. Why they called it 'pats', I dunno.

Water was pumped up from the river, from a part that never seemed to dry up, so even when there was a drought and the rest of the bush was brown, their garden was always a lovely green. When their fruit and vegetables were picked, they brought them into town by horse and dray and sold them to the shops and people of Moree.

There were five Chinese men. The one who spoke pidgin English looked after the shed in town and did all the selling and the other four, who did all the growing, only spoke Chinese.

I liked the Chinese because they always seemed to be happy, talking and laughing all the time, even when they were eating from their little bowls that they held right up to their mouths and pushed the food in with their chopsticks. They were pretty good to us because Brian and me used to collect all the old leaves from the cabbages and lettuces for Brownie and the chooks and often they'd give us a pile of 'specks',

y'know, fruit that was only a little bit rotten. We'd just cut the rotten bit out and eat the rest.

I didn't like raiding their garden. It didn't seem right because they were friendly and would always talk to me and roar with laughter. I didn't know what they said most of the time, but it seemed nice. Also, I'd have to say I'd been stealing at my next confession, like the last time we'd raided their garden and I went to confession . . .

'I stole twice, Father.'

'You know it's a sin to steal. Can you put what you stole back?'

'No, Father. They were watermelons and I ate 'em.'

'Yes . . . er . . . Well, you must make an Act of Perfect Contrition and promise not to do it again.'

'Yes, Father.'

And here I was, off again to have another go at stealing watermelons. But if I didn't go, Bluey and Mick would think I wasn't game.

'Can you see anybody, Bluey?'

'No. They must all be in the house.'

We were at the rabbit-proof fence that went right round the garden. On top of the fence were

three strands of barbed wire to help keep the roos and kids like us out, I suppose.

The Chinese were good gardeners. The rows and rows of vegetables were neat and straight and there weren't any weeds between the fruit trees. It must have taken a lot of hard work to keep the garden that way and everybody said that they worked like 'coolies', lived on rice, saved all their money and then went back to China to die.

That didn't seem much of a life to me, so why did they always look so happy?

We tied the dogs up in the shade of a tree.

The only place to get over the fence out of sight of the house was in the corner behind some orange trees. Getting back was easy because the corner-post was propped up from the inside by another one and you just ran up it and over.

By pushing down on the rabbit-wire and pulling up the first strand of barbed wire, we squeezed through and started to crawl along the ground between the orange trees and the beans. You could see the large ripe watermelons in the distance at the end of the row of beans and you had to crawl in such a way so as not to make any dust in case anybody was watching.

Bluey said we had to be extra careful because he'd heard they had shotguns loaded with saltpetre in case anybody tried to steal from their garden.

I was crawling so slowly I didn't seem to be getting anywhere.

'Come on, Snow! Hurry up!' whispered Bluey.

It was alright for Bluey and Mick—they were behind me. I was the first in and I'd be the last one out.

To take my mind off shotguns and saltpetre, I started to say the Chinese ABC to myself. Well, I think it was the Chinese ABC, Bluey reckoned it was . . .

'H—I—CHICK—A—LI—CHICK—A—LI —EENEE—BUM—BUM—BEENEE—CAT—A —KIS—A—WHISKY—H—I—CHICK—A—LI —CHICK—A—LI—EENEE . . . '

We all must've been looking down because just after 'EENEE' I looked up and there were the four Chinese gardeners about twenty-five yards away, grinning at us, and one of them had a shotgun.

'Shit! Run,' yelled Bluey.

I didn't need to be told. I think I started

running before my feet touched the ground. And at the same time the Chinese started yelling and firing. I felt two sharp stings in my right leg from the first shot.

'Shit! I've been shot. Hurry up, Bluey,' I yelled.

'Hurry up, Mick!' yelled Bluey.

When I was halfway up the post the extra sharp stings in my bum from the second shot made me slip and I landed on the barbed wire. I could feel it tearing my right arm as I rolled off it onto the ground outside the fence.

We collected the dogs and didn't stop running till we were out of breath and out of range and hiding under the roots of a big gum tree on the river bank. I stood in the river till I stopped bleeding.

There was a neat hole in my right arm the size of a threepenny bit. It was so clean and round it looked like it had been done with a brace and bit. Bluey got the two pieces of salt-petre out of my right calf muscle with his hunting knife.

'Snow, the two in yer bum're too deep. Yer'll have to get yer mum to get it out with a long needle.'

'Shit, Bluey. How do I tell Mum I've got salt-petre in me bum? Saltpetre isn't something sharp you sit on, like a tack. How do I tell Mum I sat on saltpetre and it went in about half an inch?'

As Mum squeezed and pricked the saltpetre out of my bottom, she said, 'You'll have to go to confession.'

I was spending an awful lot of time at confession these days. Maybe I was just going through a bad time like other ten year olds.

I knelt down all the time I was waiting my turn for Father Tuttle to hear my confession because the saltpetre holes in my bottom hadn't healed properly and they were still itching from the iodine and meths that Mum kept putting on to stop them getting poisoned. If I sat for too long I started to wriggle about a lot, like I had St Vitus's Dance.

'In the name of the Father and of the Son and of the Holy Ghost, Amen. It's two weeks since my last confession, Father. I missed sayin' my mornin' prayers, twice, and I had bad inten-tions, Father.'

Please, I thought, don't let him ask 'bad intentions about what?' because then I'd have to

tell him 'bad intentions about watermelons', and then he might remember the time I stole them before and I'd promised not to do it again. But all he said was, 'For your penance, say five Our Fathers and five Hail Marys. Now make an Act of Perfect Contrition.'

Maybe he had a lot of kids coming in and saying they had 'bad intentions'. Bad intentions were when you intended to do something but you never did it, so that when you went to confession, you didn't have to say 'stealing' or 'cheating'. You just said 'bad intentions' hoping the priest wouldn't say, 'To do what, my son? Bad intentions to do what?'

I kept away from collecting the cabbage and lettuce leaves for about two weeks. Brian had been doing it but one afternoon he had to do something else and Brownie needed to eat.

'You'll have to go and face them,' Mum said. 'They probably won't recognise you. They mightn't even be there. Anyway, I told you to go and say you were sorry.'

I was filling the chaff bag as quickly as I could, hoping none of the gardeners was around when I saw eight feet pushing their way through the leaves.

Oh shit!

I looked up at four smiling Chinese. One of them leaned down and took hold of a handful of my hair and started to speak to his friends who were talking and nodding. My bloody blond hair, they'd remembered!

One man lifted up his arms as though firing a gun and said, 'Boom Boom,' then pointed at me.

I think he was asking if I got hit when they fired. Anyway, I wasn't the only fair-haired boy in Moree. I don't know why but I nodded and said, 'Yeah, I was the one yer shot.'

I don't think they understood what I said but they knew what I meant.

One started pointing to my body and saying something in Chinese. They wanted to know where?

I showed them the two scars on my leg, pointed to my bottom and made a couple of little circles with my fingers the size of a sixpence and for good luck showed them the large scab on my right arm.

This made them talk very loudly and they kept pointing at my feet and raising their arms saying, 'Boom Boom.' They were trying to tell

me that they were only aiming at my feet when they fired. I knew that anyway. It's much easier to hit somebody's back than their legs.

Still talking, they went away.

I'd just about filled the bag when they all came back and one of them handed me a sugar bag. It weighed a ton. It was full of fruit and the biggest watermelon I'd ever seen.

I looked up at four smiling faces.

'Thank you,' I said. 'I won't steal from you again.'

And each one gave a little bow and said, 'So solly,' just like they do in the movies.

I like the Chinese.

MOVING ON

Tᴇᴀ ᴀᴛ ɴɪɢʜᴛ was what we all looked forward to of a day. It was when the whole family sat around the kitchen table, my big brother Brian, my younger brothers, Clete and Joe, and my younger sisters, Moya and Noni. There was always a great smell of cooking. Mum would be busy getting it all ready and everybody would be talking at once, of what they were going to do tomorrow, of what they did today.

Dad would just sit there puffing away at his pipe, maybe with the youngest on his knee, and every now and then there'd be a hiss of steam as he spat into the fire. He only did it when we had a fire, I think he liked the sound of it, and Mum would say, 'Oh Alf, and in front of the children.'

'Sorry Beez,' he'd say.

I wished I could spit like him, he did it

between his front teeth. It wasn't a nasty spit, it sort of made a clean *phisst* and then a *hisss* as it hit the fire. He never missed.

And Mum. Most kids I know think their mum's the best, but my mum ... well, I'd back her against any of them. She worked from early in the morning until late at night, cleaning, cooking, washing, never complaining and always with a smile, 'making do' patching clothes and sending us off to school shining and clean. 'Cleanliness is next to godliness' she would often say. Maybe that's why I ended up being an altar boy—I was so clean.

At least I was at the start of the day anyhow.

My mum's smile was like, I dunno, it was kind of a gentle smile, just like her. Sometimes when she looked at you and smiled it made you want to cry and so to hide that you'd rush over and bury your head in her dress. She seemed to have so much love for all of us and always had time to show it. If you were near her she'd ruffle your hair or give you a pat or a gentle smack on your rump. I suppose we were like puppy dogs.

Yeah, I'd back my mum against anybody's.

'Alright, tea's ready. Has everybody washed their hands, Brian, Vince, Clete, Joe?'

Never Moya or Noni—didn't girls get dirty hands?

Mum said Grace then, as Dad said, 'all hell broke loose'. He reckoned that me and Brian were two of the fastest eaters in Moree; his favourite words to me at the table were, 'Do you want a shovel, Vince?' No matter how much food Mum cooked, there was never any left and the only reason Brian and me ate so fast was because if you finished first, you could scrape the dishes.

Dad finished his meal, loosened his belt and said, 'I've got somethin' to say to you all. Your mother and I have decided to move to Sydney. I've been made a senior linesman and offered a job at Ryde in Sydney. We think you would all have a better chance of gettin' good jobs there when yer leave school. If we stay here, you boys will end up being drovers and spendin' the rest of your days in the bush. You're twelve Brian and Vince is eleven, it's time we made a move.'

Everybody started talking at once.

'When do we go?'

'Where are we goin' to live?'

'What about Brownie?'

'Can we take the dogs and cats?'

'What school will we be goin' to?'

Dad shouted above the noise, 'Quiet.'

Silence.

'We won't be takin' any of the animals with us. It wouldn't be fair to the dogs to be cooped up in a city, they're used to runnin' in the bush, chasin' rabbits. They need plenty of space, and we'll have to sell Brownie and the chooks.'

'Dad, can't I take Bindy?'

'No Vince, you can't. I've already spoken to Mr Morgan and he says he'll give yer thirty shillings for her. Now I don't want any arguments.'

I rushed out of the kitchen, through the house to the front verandah, where I slept. I couldn't stop crying. I pushed my face hard into the pillow to stop the sounds I was making.

Not take Bindy?

And what about Brownie? No more hunting and swimming at the Three Mile with Bluey Baker and Mick Ellis, or going out to the slaughterhouse to see Ossie Nell and his sister, Nora . . .

What would Nora say? Nora was my girlfriend.

Well, I think she was my girlfriend. Anyway, she was the only one who hadn't laughed at me because I was wearing sandshoes at the school dance at the School of Arts hall. I didn't have any leather shoes and Mum said the sandshoes would be alright, better than the big boots with the thick rubber soles. Dad used to use the rubber from car tyres. Mum had cleaned the sandshoes with whiting. They were an old pair of Brian's and too big, and the whiting came off on my black socks. I couldn't slide on the floor because of the rubber soles, and when I danced I had to do a sort of hop. All the other kids had laughed and said I looked like a kangaroo, except Nora Nell. She had every dance with me, so I reckoned she was my girl. Anyway she was the prettiest girl at school.

I wouldn't be an altar boy any more, or get out of school every time there was a funeral, or be taken by Father Tuttle to the big sheep stations to serve Mass.

I don't know how long Mum had been there, I could feel her hand rubbing my hair, she just sat there not saying a word, the tears running down her cheeks.

'This afternoon we're all going out to the cemetery to put some flowers on John's grave. It's our last day in Moree and it's probably the last time we'll be able to see his grave.'

'What time are we gunna go, Mum?'

'We'll leave about one o'clock. We mustn't be late back.'

I don't think any of us minded going out to see the grave. John had been a nice little kid with a funny laugh like someone gargling when they've got a sore throat.

It was a two-mile walk to the cemetery and everybody we passed knew where we were going because we were all dressed-up and Mum was carrying a big bunch of flowers. Dad told everybody anyway, and promised four or five people who had someone buried out there that we'd weed the graves for them. I knew who'd have to do all the weeding—me and Brian.

John had died when he was fourteen months old of gastroenteritis; he'd been sick for about a week. I dunno why, but I came home one day from school at playtime. I never did before. Dad was home. He was sitting on the back step crying. I'd never seen him cry before

and anyway you don't expect to see your dad crying.

'John has just died,' he said, and lifted me onto his lap and held me and squeezed me, hard.

'Where's Mum, Dad?'

'She's lyin' down on the front verandah.'

'Can I go and see her?'

'Yeah, but don't worry her.'

I went out to the front verandah. Mum was lying on one of the beds; she wasn't crying but she had been, I could tell by her red eyes. She was just staring at the vine that grew across the front of the verandah. I went over to her and she reached out and put her arm around me and made room for me beside her. I cuddled into her and gave her a kiss.

'Where's John, Mum?'

'He's in the bedroom.'

'Did it sort of hurt him when he died?'

'No, he just gave a little sigh.'

'When I dropped him on his head a couple of weeks ago do you think that made him sick and helped to kill him?'

'No, Vince. That had nothing to do with him dying, it was gastroenteritis.' She didn't say any more and just held me tight.

A couple of weeks ago, I'd been giving John a ride on my shoulders and the faster I ran the more he laughed. I tripped and he shot straight off my shoulders and landed on his head on the hard gravel. He didn't make much noise, he didn't seem able to get his breath. I picked him up and ran with him in to Mum. She walked up and down with him and kept patting him on the back. Then somehow he got his breath back and started yelling. Mum had said that was a good sign.

'Mum, will I go and tell the others?'

'No, not yet. Leave them at school, I've got a lot to do.'

That afternoon we said our last goodbye to John. He was in the sitting room, in a little wooden coffin and we went in one by one and kissed him. He was dressed up in his best clothes, all in white. He looked like a clean, shiny doll. He didn't look dead at all, he just seemed like he was asleep, and when I kissed him I sort of expected him to wake up and give that funny laugh of his. Then we all knelt around the coffin and said the Rosary.

The undertaker put the lid on the coffin and it was taken to the church and put in the centre aisle on a small table. Four big candles were lit

and placed around it. We stayed in the church and prayed for a bit until Dad said someone would have to stay on watch all the time, until the funeral service the next day.

'Vince, yer better milk Brownie. Brian, you feed the chooks and dogs and collect the eggs. I'll stay over here for the first couple of hours and then one of yer come back and take over from me.'

All the work had been done and the younger ones were in bed. Brian and me were having some tea.

'I'd better go and take over from Dad,' Brian said. 'And Snow, in a couple of hours, you come over and do yer turn.'

While us kids were washing up, Mum started crying again. She'd be alright for a while and then suddenly she would start again and didn't seem to be able to stop.

I hadn't cried at all yet.

The church was dark, except for the four big candles that made dancing shadows all over the place. I said some Our Fathers and Hail Marys for John's soul, so that it would go to Heaven. But I don't think he needed them because he'd been baptised, which took away

his original sin, and he couldn't have committed any sins anyway because he was only fourteen months when he died. I suppose he'd be like one of those baby angels that were in the pictures and windows in the church. Little fat, curly-headed babies with wings coming out of their shoulders, and all the prayers we said helped them to have a better time up there.

It was strange to think that John was locked up in that little wooden box only two feet away from me. Well, his body was there but his soul left his body as soon as he died and went straight to Heaven. In some holy books, they showed the soul as looking like a football with two wings on it.

If John hadn't been baptised, he'd have gone to Limbo and never would have got to Heaven. No matter how much you prayed, it didn't do any good: he would have to stay in Limbo forever. If anybody died in a state of venial sin, they went to Purgatory and that's where your prayers did a lot of good, but if you died in a state of mortal sin you went straight to Hell and stayed there for Eternity. I knew all this because we had catechism every morning at school and Father Tuttle would

come over and test us to see that we got it all right.

It was a bit scary in the church, the candle-light flickered over the statues and somehow it seemed to make them move. I could just see some of the pictures of the Stations of the Cross—'The Crowning with Thorns', 'The Nailing to the Cross', 'The Carrying of the Cross' and 'The Dying on the Cross'.

When the Stations of the Cross were said, us altar boys used to carry candles and we would each bet a penny that we could keep our candle alight till we got back to the vestry. You had to protect the flame with your hand from the wind made by three big electric fans above the centre aisle. Mum reckoned I never paid any attention during the Stations of the Cross. Well you couldn't really, it was a pretty hard job keeping that candle alight, the wind seemed to come in all directions. I've won as much as fivepence in one go.

It was so quiet and the candles were making shadows across the large crucifix at the side of the altar. Christ looked like he was moving, you know, squirming from the pain in his hands and feet from the nails.

I was starting to get goose pimples and a bit

frightened; I thought I heard something just then, at the back of the church. I looked around, nothing, only shadows. Maybe if I said some prayers it might help. Yeah, I'll say some Our Fathers and Hail Marys for John so that he can have a better time in Heaven. I curled up on the seat, closed my eyes and started praying, 'Our Father who art in Heaven, hallowed be thy name . . .'

A gentle hand woke me up.

'You can go home now, Vince.'

'Alright, Mum. Goodnight.'

She put her arms around me and kissed me. Then she made a sort of choking noise and started to cry.

Father Tuttle said I didn't have to toll the bell for John if I didn't want to. But I did want to because it would be my way of saying goodbye.

Dong! Dong! Dong! Dong!

I could feel the goose pimples coming out on my arms.

'John, Mum said me droppin' you had nothin' to do with yer dyin' . . . but she might be just sayin' that.'

Now the tears were starting to come into my eyes.

Dong! Dong! Dong!

I got angry and started hitting the bell
harder and harder and faster and faster as if I
was trying to reach John and tell him through
the tolling that I was ...

Sorry! Sorry! Sorry! Sorry!

Not many came to the funeral next day. There
was the hearse and three cars. We all went in a
Ford.

Everybody started crying again when the
coffin was lowered into the grave. Father Tuttle
said some nice things about us and young John,
and how he was sure John was in Heaven, and
then we all threw some earth onto the coffin.
The gravedigger, who had been standing behind
Father Tuttle, started shovelling the earth back
into the grave. Dad had his arm around Mum
and he took her away so she couldn't look.
There was still one tiny bit of the coffin showing
and as the next shovelful covered it, I started to
cry ... properly.

But now, when we went to see his grave, we
didn't cry. We were sorry that he was dead but
we just didn't cry any more, because Mum said
he was in Heaven with all the angels having a
good time and he'd be alright.

IN

LOVING MEMORY

OF

JOHN

PATRICK BALL,

DIED 7TH DEC 1933,

AGED 14 MONTHS.

R.I.P.

It was a little mound of earth with a headstone. We cleared all the weeds and Mum put the new flowers on it. Then we knelt down and said the Rosary. We always said the Rosary, we said it for everything: in the drought, when anybody was sick, when they got better, and even when Brownie was having a calf.

It took us about an hour to weed the other graves and tidy them up a bit.

Then we all went home.

The last few weeks had been real busy.

Dad went to Sydney to look for a place to live. Brownie had been sold to Mr McCauley. What would Mr McCauley do with all that milk? They didn't have any children and Mr McCauley was so fat anyway, they couldn't drink it all.

Mum had sold most of the chooks. The rest we ate. I killed and plucked one every day for dinner. I like chicken better than rabbit.

I was glad in a way it was all over, because I don't think I could cry any more ...

Brownie, Bindy, Nora Nell.

Nora Nell had stood on the top step of their back verandah winding a plait of her hair around her finger. She had a real pretty frock on and looked all golden with those lovely little freckles on her nose. She just stood there looking at me as I told her that Sydney wasn't very far away and, anyway, one day I'd be coming back to see her and I was gunna be a cowboy on the fillums, and be famous and maybe take her to Hollywood. I was hoping she'd say, 'I'll wait for you,' like they do on the pictures, but she didn't. She stared at me and then stepped down and kissed me on the cheek and ran inside. Never said nothing. Not even goodbye. I looked after her for a bit hoping she'd come back, then I turned and ran.

It was only after I'd got past the big gum tree that I started bawling.

'Vince, I'm sure Mr Morgan won't mind

you keeping Bindy for another day, he's a nice man, just go and ask him.'

I ran all the way to the grocery shop, where Mr Morgan was out the back weighing up sugar.

'Mr Morgan, can I just keep Bindy for another day? I'll bring her round to the shop tomorrow arvo. Would that be alright?'

He looked at me for a bit, nodded and said, 'Yeah, okay Snow, tomorrow.'

'Thanks Mr Morgan.'

We were leaving for Sydney the day after tomorrow and I wanted to keep her as long as I could.

She was six weeks old when Dad brought her home.

'Just look after her, Snow. Treat her right and she'll be a real friend.'

As I held that pot-bellied, wriggling bundle of puppy in my arms and as the whole family *ooh'd* and *aah'd*, patted and stroked her, she peed all over me. Must have been the excitement, I suppose.

'What'll yer call her?' asked Brian.

'Dunno.'

Then I noticed a couple of bindi-eyes sticking to her hair.

'I think I'll call her "Bindy".'

'Odd kind of name,' said Dad. 'But she's your dog, call her what you like.'

We sort of grew up together, Bindy and me. I think the only time we were apart was when I was at school or Mass. Every afternoon after school, I'd head straight for the shed to let her off the chain and when she spotted me, she'd start jumping and barking and getting so excited that I reckoned one day she'd pull the shed down or choke herself. I'd let her off the chain and then it would start, one happy dog leaping all over me trying to lick me to death, then racing around in circles, scattering our sixty-odd chooks in all directions. Mum used to reckon it put them off laying.

Bindy never changed over all those years, just grew bigger, that's all. She didn't know, mind or care if I was in trouble at school, home or anywhere. She was just happy to see me. I reckon she loved me. I know I loved her. I wasn't sure really what loving was or whether loving a dog was the same as loving your family, or the sort of loving I used to see at the pictures, you know, with Tom Mix and Buck Jones, when, at the end of the picture, they got the girl and

started kissing and stuff and rode off into the distance.

I watched Bindy gulp down her favourite meal of liver and scraps. It was the last one I'd be cooking for her and, as always, she cleaned her dish in about thirty seconds. I'm a pretty fast eater too—maybe that's who I learned it from!

'I won't be seein' you after tomorrow, Bindy. Dad's takin' us all to Sydney. He reckons we'd be better off down there and the place where we'll be livin' is pretty small, with only a tiny yard. He says you'd be better off stayin' in Moree.'

She just looked at me, cocked her ears and wagged her tail. I don't think she understood what I was saying but I felt I had to say goodbye to her, talk to her, tell her how much I was gunna miss her, talk about all the great times we'd had over the years, swimming at the Three Mile, hunting rabbits, looking for Brownie. I just kept talking. I don't really know what about, just patting her head and talking. Mostly about the bush I suppose, because that's the place we both loved and where we had the best times.

I dunno if it was the sound of my voice and

the stroking of her head but she became very
still, just lay there looking at me.

'Bindy, I'm never gunna have another dog,
'cos it would never be as good as you. Anyway
who wants a dog in Sydney? And don't go givin'
Mr Morgan any trouble . . . and look after yourself, do yer hear?'

I gave her a big hug and that's when I
started bawling. I know she knew what was happening. I know she did and I don't care what
anybody says.

I felt a gentle touch on my shoulder.

'Come and have your tea, Vince. It's getting
late.' Mum leaned over and patted Bindy and
said, 'There's a good girl.'

Next day, Bindy and I walked past Mr Morgan's shop five times before I took her in. If she
hadn't kept looking at me and sort of shivering,
I would have been alright.

I gave Bindy to Mr Morgan in front of the
grocery counter. She just looked at me. I turned
and ran, knocking over a pile of IXL jams on the
way out.

I couldn't see too good . . .

I suppose I was a bit of a sis. I'll bet
cowboys like Buck Jones and Tim McCoy didn't

cry. Well, not in front of people, anyway.

Bluey and Mick had come to the station to see me off.

All Mick said was, 'See yer, Snow.'

And Bluey with a grin on his face, 'That's for the snakes in Sydney.' He gave me his shanghai.

Snakes in Sydney? Bluey must be joking, there wouldn't be snakes anywhere that there are lots of people. Snakes are more frightened of us than we are of them. They get out of your way pretty quick, unless of course you bail them up, or step on them, then they'd have a go at you.

Living in the bush they somehow became part of your life. As long as I can remember, Mum and Dad have been saying, 'And watch out for snakes', and I suppose you did, without thinking.

The first time I saw a snake was underneath the mulberry tree in our backyard when we were living in Wee Waa. It was Moya's birthday and Mum had laid the table out there.

'It will be nice and cool,' she said.

The party was real good—until Moya yelled, 'There's a snake under my chair!'

And there was. A big black one. We ran for our lives in all directions yelling 'Snake!'

Mum and Dad came running out of the house. Dad shouting, 'Everybody get inside while I kill it. Which way did it go?'

'It was goin' towards the tree,' said Brian.

'No it wasn't, it was just sittin' under my chair,' said Moya.

'It was after the food that we dropped from the table,' I said.

Anyway, Dad didn't kill it because he couldn't find it. I'll bet that old snake got as big a fright as we did and went for its life.

Five days later, Dad was bitten on the leg.

We were all out on the back verandah, it was a hot night and that was the only place where we could get a bit of a breeze. Dad was sitting on the step nursing Noni, who was just a baby. Suddenly he jumped about two feet in the air, slapped his leg and yelled, 'Snake! I've been bitten!'

And once again the Ball family took off, plus two dogs and a cat. It was like a madhouse. The dogs were barking, the cat meowing, and all of us yelling and falling about in the dark, trying to get the gauze door open to the kitchen. Mum

got in first and turned up the kerosene lamps.

'Has anyone else been bitten? Brian?'

'No.'

'Moya?'

'No.'

Dad by this time had given Noni to Mum, rolled his trousers up and wrapped his belt around his leg just above the bite to stop the poison going up into his body. The fang marks were just above his knee, two neat little holes like pinpricks.

'I'll take the mare,' Dad said.

He didn't even bother to saddle her, just threw the bridle over her head, hopped onto her back and cantered off to the hospital.

A week later, he came home looking as big and brown as ever. To me, Dad always looked big and brown.

I reckon it was the same snake that came to Moya's party. Dad seemed to think it slid down the passionfruit vine that covered the verandah post. If it had bitten Noni, she would have just cried a bit. Babies are always doing that, and so Mum would have taken her and rocked her or changed her nappy, or fed her, until she stopped. Then I suppose, she just would have died.

The blacktracker at Moree told me that if you kept staring into the eyes of a snake, it wouldn't move. Well, it might work for him but I never took any chances. Whenever I came face-to-face with a snake, I didn't waste any time staring at it, I just killed it.

Maybe it's true what he said, because Mum was drying-up in the kitchen one day in Moree when she looked down and saw a big black snake curled up in a patch of sunlight on the floor. She screamed, dropped the plate she was wiping and ran to the front gate and started calling out to old Mr Spicer who lived across the road. While she was doing this she happened to look down and there curled up beside the gate-post was another black snake. Mum just stared at the snake and the snake just stared at her. I dunno how long she kept that up but in the end she couldn't stand it any longer and looked up to see if Mr Spicer was coming. She heard a bit of a rustle and when she looked down again, the snake had gone.

In one year in Moree, forty snakes were seen in our yard, either going into the hedge, coming out of the well or going under the house. Maybe it was the same snake just going round in circles.

The chooks used to lay their eggs under the house and it was me and Brian's job to collect them. You had to crawl for about ten yards in the dark, and it was a bit scary. Brian was collecting them one day and he arrived at the nest at the same time as a snake. Snakes like eggs. Brian got such a fright he loosened three of the floorboards in the hall with his head!

After that Dad decided he'd put down some poison milk and kill the snakes off. I dunno whether he killed any or not, but he did kill three of Mum's best chooks.

I'd have to think up new ways of earning money in Sydney because the saddler in Moree used to pay us two and six for every snakeskin over four feet long. He'd make belts and hatbands out of them. Bluey, Mick, Bindy and me used to spend hours hunting for them and when we were lucky and found one, we'd just belt it behind the head with a stick and break its back. Once their back is broken, snakes can't chase you.

Dad said we'd be living right in Sydney, so I don't suppose there'd be many snakes about. Anyway, it wouldn't be the same without Bluey, Mick and Bindy, and I don't suppose the cityites would like chasing snakes.

I pressed my face hard against the window of the train, staring at the ground as we sped towards Sydney. Maybe I could just see one for the last time, sunning itself on a log or making its way to the rabbit-holes or curled up at the foot of a tree or by the railway track.

They said the Sydney train goes at about fifty miles an hour. I don't know what speed it was going at but it seemed to be whizzing along. As I looked out the window, hoping to spot a few roos and emus as well, I sort of felt that this would be the last time I would really see the bush.

What I saw most of from the train were rabbits. Golly, the number of rabbits we must have eaten in Moree. We always seemed to be eating rabbits, fried, stewed, roasted, baked, ever since Dad had said, 'There's a Depression on, so we'll have to live on a lot of rabbits. Vince, you're a pretty good shot with a shanghai, you keep yer mother supplied with them.'

The rabbits would squat at the bottom of the gum trees to get out of the hot sun and you could just walk up to them until you got to about twelve feet away, then aim your shanghai. When the stone hit the rabbits between the eyes,

they gave a little jump and lay there shivering. You just picked them up by the hind legs, hit them a couple of times behind the ears with the side of your hand—it was called a 'rabbit punch'—until they died. Then you stuck your hunting knife in their neck to make them bleed.

Bluey had showed me how to do that. Good old Bluey, I'll miss him, we'd become mates soon after I'd arrived from Wee Waa. He'd taught me other things as well, like bird-nesting, the best part of the river to swim in, where to steal fruit and not get caught, how to make a shanghai. Yeah, living in Moree without Bluey wouldn't have been much fun.

Mum was always saying, 'I don't know about you running around with that Bluey Baker. I think he's a bad influence on you. I hardly ever see him at Mass and I don't think his parents go at all.'

I knew he didn't go to Mass as much as me and maybe he was in a 'state of mortal sin' most of the time for not going to Mass on Sundays, but you couldn't tell. He didn't look different having his soul 'blackened by sin' all the time. He was only ten and I reckon him knowing all about the bush and being able to say poems

about wild horses like 'Rocky Ned' and knowing all the words of 'Clancy of the Overflow' and 'Who let the sliprails down' made up for it. I'd never been able to learn them and say them like Bluey could. And he'd always seem to turn up when you were in trouble, he would just be there, like years ago, when . . .

'Bluey, I've gotta get back. I said I'd be home about three and anyway it looks like a storm's comin' up.'

'Cripes Snow, it's too early to go home yet. You can go if you want to, but me and Mick's stayin'.'

The three of us had been hunting all day and were cooling off with a swim at the Three Mile. I'd told Mum I'd be home fairly early to help Brian cut branches at Mrs Wild's. Because of the drought there wasn't much grass around for Brownie and me and Brian would offer to cut back people's trees if we could have the branches for an extra bit of feed. Also, it'd been one of those weeks when I always seemed to be in trouble and I didn't want to make things worse by not turning up.

'Yeah, well I'm goin'.'

'Okay, Snow. Don't get lost. Head for the

old slaughterhouse and then just keep goin'.'

Get lost, what's he talking about? Of course I won't get lost. I know I hadn't been in this part of the bush before and it was only my second time out with Bluey, but I'd be right.

I'd been walking for about a mile and the strong wind was starting to howl and blow dust, leaves, branches and roly-polies across the plains. It was just like a dust storm and the black clouds covering the whole sky made it pretty dark. I could hardly see where I was going and the wind was so strong that I had to lean into it to stop from being blown over. Then it started to rain.

It was like what you see on the pictures— the lost, frightened, little boy battling the wind and the rain trying to find his way home—taking shelter in the forest where all the trees have strange and frightening shapes. Animals appear suddenly, scream and cry out, an owl just looking, a snake sliding by. But in the pictures the boy was always brave and didn't cry, and then Rin Tin Tin or some other clever animal would find him and lead him back or get help and everybody lived happily ever after.

I didn't own a Rin Tin Tin or a clever animal that would find me. What do I do? Wait

until the storm passes over or what? It was really dark now and I was pretty scared, because the wind and rain was so strong it was bringing branches crashing down and I was frightened I was gunna get hit. I was lost. I didn't know where the slaughterhouse was, I didn't even know which way the town was. But I'm not gunna cry and be a sis, I'll be like Buck Jones when he was seven years old. Yeah, I'll bet he was brave and didn't cry. I'll squat at the butt of a big gum tree and wait.

I dunno how long I was there. I was day-dreaming, just staring out at the rain, hoping it would stop and that the wind would die down. I must have closed my eyes because suddenly there were two small figures standing right in front of me. It took me a few seconds to make out who they were. I'd been thinking of Buck Jones and trying not to cry.

'You silly bugger, Snow. You went the wrong way. We thought we'd better follow you in case you got lost ... and you did,' said Bluey. 'We'll head for the slaughterhouse and then we'll be right.'

I know I didn't have a Rin Tin Tin, but I did have Bluey for a mate.

three

CITYITES AND
PADDED CELLS

NUMBER 625 DARLING Street, Rozelle, Sydney, was our new home. It was above a grocery shop called Derrin Brothers. The backyard was a tiny piece of hard, black earth, no grass or trees, just a lot of rubbish from the shop. The dunny was in the yard too.

The house was dark. In one room there weren't even any windows.

Mum and Dad didn't say much when we arrived. Mum made a cup of tea and the whole family just looked out of the front window at the trams, taxis and lorries. Every time a tram went by the whole house shook and even when the windows were closed the noise was still loud. Dad said the trams stopped running at twelve and started in the morning at five, but we'd get used to it, he said.

We all just seemed to sit around for the first

week. Dad had taken his holidays at the same time as the school holidays so that we wouldn't miss any school when we moved. He'd sit puffing at his pipe, looking out of the bedroom window at the trams. I suppose he was thinking about Wee Waa and Moree, about the quiet. He was born at Werris Creek and brought up in the bush. He missed it as much as we did.

And we all missed having a verandah, where in the evenings after all the tea things had been washed up, we'd gather and talk. Dad didn't talk much in the evenings now. Not like it was in Wee Waa and Moree, where every summer's night was the same—we'd have tea, wash up and then Mum would say, 'Where will we say the Rosary?'

'The verandah,' four voices would answer.

And no matter who was there, they had to join in. Mum would always offer it up for something. To a special saint, like St Anthony, if something valuable was lost. He was supposed to help you find it. Sometimes it worked and sometimes it didn't.

When Dad was going on one of his trips into the bush, we'd offer it up to St Christopher, the saint who looked after travellers, or to help

somebody who was sick get better. Most times it would be for one of our relatives who was ill. We said it for Uncle Nick for six months once. He'd fallen into a threshing machine and got cut up something terrible. Mum reckoned it was our prayers that helped save him.

We offered it up for Brownie to have a heifer calf and not a bull calf. And the priest was always asking us to pray for him, because when you were in confession and after you'd said your Act of Contrition and he'd given you your penance and absolution, he'd always say 'Pray for me', just before you left.

I wonder why he always said that? You'd think he'd be holy enough, wouldn't you? And wouldn't need your prayers.

I know I shouldn't have, but I used to pray for other things as well, and I know Brian and Dad did too. I always offered up a week's Rosaries just before the annual sports day, and I reckon it did some good, because I won the 100 yards five years on the trot. And then there were all the other things to pray for, like making Nora Nell like me better than Mick Ellis, and helping Bindy win the maiden stakes at the showground.

We were so used to saying Our Fathers and

Hail Marys that we'd rattle them off without really thinking about what we were saying or keeping proper count of them. Brian and me were always getting them wrong—he got up to fifteen Hail Marys one night before Mum stopped him. You were only supposed to say ten in each decade. Somehow, the low noise of all of us praying used to send Dad off to sleep, and when it was his turn to say a decade there'd be a silence and Mum would say, 'Alf!', then Dad would give a jump and start his Our Fathers off with a rush.

Mum loved the verandah. After working all day, washing, ironing, cooking and cleaning, sitting out on the verandah was the only time she could have a rest. She'd just sit there staring out at the blackness of the night. And every now and then Dad would give an extra hard puff on his pipe and the glow would give enough light to show the whole family. I think he did it on purpose so he could count us and make sure we were all there.

Mum said she loved this part of the day. She said it was the quietness. And on the bright moonlight nights, and if you were sitting in the right place, Mum's face looked all smooth and

shiny. She didn't look tired any more. She looked young and pretty, and often Dad would reach out and touch her.

'Are yer alright, Beez?'

'Yes, Alf.'

Dad always asked her that.

You could hear the noise of the crickets from the clump of trees, and the croaks of the frogs from the well, and all the strange calls and noises that made up the sounds of the bush.

Dad was a linesman, which meant he put up telegraph poles. Sometimes he would go away for about six weeks, and of an evening when he got back, he'd puff away on his pipe and tell us yarns of the drovers and boundary riders who he'd met, and the bush stories that had been carried in from the outback by the 'Mulga Wire' or bush telegraph. We'd sit there listening to every word he said, and you sort of felt happy. I don't mean laughing, you just felt good, and every now and then you'd get your hair ruffled by Mum. If you were out of her reach you moved a bit closer so as you wouldn't miss out.

Some nights, Dad would recite a few of our favourite poems and after a while, in a kind of

dream, I became 'Clancy of the Overflow' battling with the flooded river, or 'The Man from Snowy River', never giving in as I raced my pony down the mountain after the wild bush horses. *'And the Man from Snowy River never shifted in his seat, it was grand to see that mountain horseman ride.'*

I might have been like him and Clancy if we hadn't come to Sydney.

And other nights, Dad would tell us of the war when he was with the Lighthorse in Egypt, about France and England. Of being wounded in the knee, the trenches, the mud, of going over the top and the nice English nurse he met in hospital. He always told that bit, and Mum would throw her head back and break the stillness with her nice laugh.

In our new house there was nowhere to play. We didn't know anybody in Rozelle and all the boys in the street seemed to knock about in gangs. Being a good Catholic family, Friday night was fish and chip night. To begin with, me and Brian used to fight to see who would go to buy them because you'd get a pennyworth of scraps for yourself and pinch a few chips on the way home.

After being bailed up a couple of times by the street gangs and coming home without the chips, Dad decided to take over. Well, it was pretty hard to fight off about six kids with an armful of fish and chips.

Dad said that we'd have to pull our belts in, that living in Sydney would cost a lot more money. In Moree we had Brownie, grew our own vegetables, had fruit trees, chooks, eggs— and all those rabbits. Dad said Brian and me would have to take a job when we were settled at school. He said there were a couple of grocery shops wanting boys for Saturday morning for delivering, and also the paper shop wanted paper boys.

Brian and me used to go bottling every Sunday morning before Mass. We'd get up at five and go around all the lanes, collecting empty beer bottles. Then we'd take them to the bottle yard and sell them, or wait for the bottle-o to come during the week. Sometimes we made as much as two shillings out of it.

Three more days to go and me and Brian would be starting at our new school, the Christian Brothers, Rozelle. Mum went to see them and it

had been alright, we were going to start next Monday. Brian had got a new pair of long 'uns, a blazer with the proper colours—red and blue— and a new pair of shoes. He'd never worn shoes before. We'd always worn boots but most of the boys in Sydney seemed to wear shoes. I wouldnt've minded a new pair of shoes to wear to school but I always got Brian's hand-me-downs, he seemed to grow faster than me and Mum would patch and wash his clothes and they'd be mine . . . until they fell apart.

We all got up extra early on Monday morning, Mum said we mustn't be late on our first day. Brian looked real nice when he was dressed in the school uniform. He was all navy, red and blue, and suddenly didn't seem to be one of us any more.

The night before, Mum had given us a bath and washed our hair. When she'd finished scrubbing us, we were so clean we sort of shone and somehow this morning we were still shining. I don't think we'd ever been so clean.

'And be good boys,' she said as she kissed us goodbye.

Mum had a sort of funny look on her face. She was smiling but somehow it was different,

maybe because her eyes seemed to be all watery. I looked back, and she was still standing at the back gate. She waved and we waved back.

The school was about a mile away if you went through the lanes. Dad said we weren't even to kick one tin on our way, and the lanes had hundreds and hundreds of them. All those tins and not allowed to kick them.

The Christian Brothers looked like priests but they weren't because they couldn't say Mass. They only taught. They were sort of like nuns, only they were men ... anyway, that's what Dad said.

Two boys walking ahead of us were dressed up just like Brian. I don't think Brian liked his uniform much because he kept tugging at his collar and fidgeting with his blazer buttons. He couldn't make up his mind whether to do up his blazer, or leave it undone. I always took an interest in Brian's clothes, because one day I knew I'd be wearing them.

I hated first days, you didn't know anybody and everybody seemed to stare at you. Dad said that he always hated first days at school too, but he said the best thing was to 'offer out' the best fighter in the class. He said it saved a lot of

trouble. If you won, all the better, but if you lost it didn't seem to matter because it showed you were 'game' and would have a 'go', and then even the bullies would leave you alone.

I remember my first day at Moree. A bit scared, I had said, 'Who's the best fighter in the class?'

A boy much smaller than me came over and said, 'I am.'

'I'll fight yer after school,' I said.

He looked at me for a bit and then said, 'Alright. Behind the tennis shed after school.'

He had bright red hair and a freckled face, his shirt was patched in front, and the patch was a different colour from the shirt. His trousers were too long for him, he didn't wear a belt, he used a piece of rope, and he was bare-footed.

'What's yer name?'

'Jimmy Baker—but everybody calls me Bluey.'

'My name's Vincent Ball and they call me Snowy.'

Everyone from school had come to watch the fight, and Brian said it was a pretty good'un while it lasted. He and Bluey had got most of the blood off me before they took me home. It's

funny how much blood can come out of your nose. I bled like a stuck pig after I'd run into Bluey's straight left. The big boys had let it go on a bit longer and then stopped it. They said Bluey was the winner.

Mum was pretty angry when she saw the mess I was in.

All Dad said was, 'I told yer to keep yer guard up and tuck yer chin into yer shoulder. Look, like this.'

He then did a bit of shadow-boxing around the kitchen until Mum stopped him. She reckoned it was all his fault for teaching us how to box. She said it encouraged us to pick fights.

It was funny, after that fight Bluey became my best friend. They'd all be going to school now at Moree, they'd be in Sister Mary Ellis's class—Nora, Bluey, Mick. I wished I was with them.

You could hear the noise from the school above the rattling of the trams. Brian and me stopped on the other side of the road and looked at the hundreds of boys shouting and talking at our first big school. There was a large cross on one wall and underneath it a sign said, CHRISTIAN BROTHERS COLLEGE, ROZELLE. I looked at

all the boys in their navy-blue blazers, school ties, socks and shoes. I was wearing boots, grey socks, short patched trousers, grey shirt and one of Brian's coats. Mum had shortened the sleeves and patched the elbows. She always said, 'It doesn't matter if your clothes are patched as long as they're *clean.*'

And Dad always made me wear braces. He said they'd make me stand up straight and stop me getting round-shouldered.

I felt like a big country bumpkin as I walked through the gates of the school. Brian was saying something about 'daydreamin' and 'gettin' run over by a bloody tram'.

We just stood around a bit. A couple of boys came up and stared at us. We stared back.

'Are yer two new boys?'

'Yeah.'

They looked at my boots and the rest of me, grinned at each other and walked away. I could feel myself getting hot all over and the patches on my trousers seemed to be growing bigger, and were burning holes in my bum. I felt that everybody in the schoolyard was looking at me.

'Let's go over and lean against the wall.'

'What for?' asked Brian.

He looked at me for a bit, then he said, 'Okay, Snow.'

We seemed to be the only new boys because everybody else was talking to each other, and they all had on proper school clothes and blazers with badges on the pockets. There was nobody else standing around like me and Brian.

'What's yer name?'

A boy of about fifteen was standing in front of us. He had a badge above his top pocket which said 'School Captain' and a piece of paper in his hand with names on it.

'Brian Ball.'

'Vincent Ball.'

'Right. Brian, you're in Brother English's class ... that's it over there. And Vincent, you're in Brother Carey's class ... it's the end room in this buildin'. I'd get over there if I were you, the bell'll be goin' soon. Hope yer like the school.'

'I wonder if Brother English is related to Father English at Moree?' said Brian. 'He might be ... See yer at lunch, Snow.'

'Yeah.'

Brian walked off to his classroom as I sort of moved sideways, keeping close to the wall, towards the room at the end of the building.

The bell rang and hundreds of boys ran in all directions. About twenty pushed past me into the room at the end. There was lots of shouting and pushing and then it was all quiet. A brother had come into the room. All the boys stood up.

'Good mornin', Bra!'

'Good morning, boys. Sit down. I believe we have a new boy, Vincent Ball. Would he come up?'

I stood up as about twenty heads turned and looked at me. I tried to keep my hands behind my back as I walked up to the brother's desk.

'I'm Brother Carey. You'll be sitting in the front row, the desk at the end.'

The roll was called, we had morning prayers and then Brother Carey told us to write a story about our holidays and he'd be back in half an hour.

Gee, I could start off by telling them about Moree and hunting and swimming at the Three Mile, about Brownie, Bindy and ... A sudden stinging pain on the back of my neck ... I'd often felt this kind of pain before. I knew it was made by a paper pellet fired by a rubber band. I turned and then they all started asking questions.

81

'Where d'yer come from?'

'Moree.'

'How old are you?'

'Eleven.'

'Can yer swim?'

'Yeah.'

'Do yer ride?'

'Yeah.'

'Are yer a good runner?'

'Yeah, pretty good.'

'Do yer play football?'

'Yeah.'

'What position?'

'On the wing. Sometimes five-eight.'

'Do yer play tennis?'

'Yeah.'

'Yer seem to be able to do everythin'. Can yer fight?'

'A bit ...'

And then, I dunno how it happened ... it sounded as if it was coming from me ... It *was* coming from me ...

'Who's the best fighter in the class?'

Why did I say that? I didn't really mean to. It just sort of came out.

'Yer a mug-lair,' one of 'em said.

'Skite,' said another.

'Country bumpkin. Who d'yer think yer are?' They all seemed to be talking at once.

'Teach him a lesson, Charlie.'

One of the boys pushed his way forward.

'I'm Charlie Bennett. I don't know whether I'm the best fighter in the class but I'll take yer on.'

He looked around the room as he said it. Nobody argued with him, so I guess he was the best fighter in the class.

We looked at each other. He was the same height as me, with dark hair and wearing all the school uniform.

'We'll go down to White Bay near the silos, after school. Just follow us,' he said.

He made it sound like he went down there quite a lot.

The essay I wrote was pretty bad. All I could think about was the fight. Trying to remember all the things Dad had taught me, learning from watching Bluey.

'Keep yer chin tucked into yer shoulder, Snow,' Bluey had said. We often used to spar for fun, never closing our fists, just pretending we were Gene Tunney and Jack Dempsey.

'Keep yer guard up and when yer throw a

left, just shoot it straight out, never pull it back to throw it. A good straight left is one of the best punches in fightin', it keeps the other bloke away. Just keep jabbin' it out.'

If anybody knew about that, it was me, remembering my first day at school in Moree, when I ran into one of Bluey's straight lefts, and all that blood.

I don't know how I got through the morning, I made so many mistakes in everything I did. Brother Carey came over to me just before lunch and wanted to know if I was alright. He said I didn't seem to be concentrating and I'd have to try harder if I wanted to keep up with the other boys.

'You've done it again, haven't yer, Snow,' said Brian. 'When I heard that there was some mug-lair offerin' out the best fighter in yer class, I knew it was you. Won't yer ever learn?'

He looked at me for a bit.

'Well, yer can't back out now,' he said. 'Yer gotta make the best of it. I'll come down and watch it. And don't rush in at the start of the fight, just take yer time. Don't stand flat-footed, keep on yer toes and yer guard up and use yer left. It's yer best punch.'

I'd bought a chip roll for lunch, and eating it in such a hurry, it now seemed to be stuck somewhere between my throat and belly. I was so nervous I didn't seem to know what I was doing.

All the advice that everybody had given me in the past kept rushing through my mind: keep on yer toes; tuck yer chin in; keep yer guard up; don't close yer eyes; use yer left. Why was I so nervous anyway? It was only a fight and I'd had plenty of those before.

If only Bluey was here. Gee, I missed him now. He'd always been around when I was having a fight and knowing that he was there and on my side somehow quietened me down. He never talked about the fight that I was going to have. He'd just sit there throwing stones at something and hitting it about nine times out of ten, talking away quietly about rabbits, hunting, the bush, what we'd do on Saturday.

He'd been my best mate for all those years, and in some strange way like a brother, only not like a brother because you could talk to Bluey about everything. Things that I wouldn't talk about to Brian.

I wish that chip roll would go all the way

down. I suppose Bluey'd be having his lunch now in Moree. Most likely eating beetroot sandwiches. I don't think he liked them much because the beetroot turned the bread pink and made it soggy.

'I'll swap yer a sandwich, Snow,' he often said. And I'd give him one of my tomato sandwiches for one of his beetroot ones. Bluey's parents grew a lot of beetroot and we grew a lot of tomatoes. Good old Bluey, with his red hair, freckled face and clothes that were always too big for him.

Nobody had talked to me during lunch time. A couple of boys from my class came over and stood near me and talked to each other in a loud voice.

'That skite from Moree should look good with a couple of black eyes. Who's the best fighter in the class? What a lair!' They walked away laughing.

The lessons in the afternoon seemed to go on for ever and all I could think about was the fight. When school was out, I followed the crowd of boys towards the silos. Brian caught up with me and asked me how I felt.

'Scared,' I said. And I was.

It wasn't much of a fight, Charlie Bennett

made the same mistake I'd made when I fought Bluey. He ran into my straight left, twice, and he bled like a stuck pig. He wasn't really hurt but there seemed to be so much blood coming from his nose that we just sort of stopped. I suppose I was the winner.

If Bluey had been there, he'd have just said, 'Good on yer, Snow.'

Mum and everybody kept asking us how we liked our new school; wanting to know about our teachers, were the lessons hard, what we had for lunch? We'd been given sixpence each. I said I'd bought a chip roll and it was real good. Brian had bought a saveloy roll, he said it was great.

Dad didn't say very much. He just kept looking at me every now and then. Mum went to get the pudding and while she was putting the dirty dishes in the sink and making a bit of a noise, Dad leaned over and asked, 'Who's the best fighter in yer class?'

'I am.'

He just sat there rocking back and forwards in his chair, nodding his head, with a bit of a grin on his face.

Lying in bed that night, I thought about the

silence and then the noise, after I'd said, 'Who's the best fighter in the class.' The silence seemed to go on for ages. I don't think I've ever been so frightened. Maybe Dad was wrong in encouraging me to 'offer out' the best fighter on my first day at school and it did make me look a bit of a mug-lair. Who'd I think I was anyway? I'm not gunna do it again.

It was my second day at my new school and I wondered how it'd go after the fight. I was a bit scared as I walked across the playground. Mum had made me promise not to fight, no matter who picked on me. Dad had been roused on and Brian was told to keep an eye on me. Some of the boys stared at me for a bit, but so far I hadn't heard 'big-head', 'mug-lair', 'country bumpkin', 'skite'.

'Do you have a nickname?'

A tall, red-headed, freckle-faced boy stood in front of me barring my way.

'Yeah. Most people call me Snow 'cos of me blond hair.'

'Yeah. Well, they call me Ginger 'cos of me red hair, Ginger Kelly.'

'Most kids I know who have red hair are called Bluey,' I said.

'Yeah. Well I'm one red-headed kid that's called Ginger. Okay?'

'Yeah. Okay,' I said quickly.

'You can go the knuckle a bit,' he said.

Aw no, not another fight, I thought. How do I back down if he picks me? Dad said I might have a bit of trouble with other kids wanting to have a go at me. Like being 'the fastest gun in the West', I suppose.

'Yeah, a bit,' I replied and just stared at him.

He stared back, then he grinned. He must've known what I was thinking because he said, 'Don't worry, I can't fight me way out of a paper bag.'

My first friend at my new school.

'G'day. My name's Jack Murphy. You're in my cricket team. We're playin' at Callan Park. Right?'

'Right,' I said. 'Where's Callan Park?'

'It's the other end of Darling Street, towards Leichhardt. It's the loony bin. We use it for athletics, cricket and football. We march up there from school on Thursday afternoon.'

It was going to be a practice match to pick the players for the class team. I hope they give

me a bowl. I wasn't a bad bowler and if I took a couple of wickets I might get in the team.

Thursday came and we set off after lunch for my first sports day at my new school. We marched up Western Road, turned left at the crossroads and went along Darling Street.

'That's Callan Park, Snow,' said Ginger, pointing to a pair of large iron gates on the other side of the road.

As we got closer I could see a guard standing behind the gates. The high brick walls, they must of been about twenty foot, stretched away into the distance on each side.

'Hey, Ginge, do the madmen walk around? Will they be walkin' around while we're playin' cricket?'

'Some of them will be—the sort of half-mad ones. The real loony ones are locked up in padded cells. I'll show you the buildin' where they are when we get in.

'Snow, don't let Brother Carey hear you callin' 'em loonies or madmen. Yer supposed to call 'em patients.'

'Righto, Ginge.'

'And don't call this place a madhouse or loony bin. It's an asylum.'

'Right. Ginge, have you ever seen a padded cell?'

'No, but they reckon that all the walls and floors are padded with some soft stuff so that when the madmen try to kill themselves by runnin' straight at the wall they don't hurt themselves.'

'Honest?'

'Yeah.'

'Gee whiz.'

The guard opened a small iron gate next to the big ones and we all walked through. The brick walls looked bigger than ever and on top of them I could just see the sharp points of broken bottles. You'd cut yourself to pieces if you tried to get over them. Most of the others said 'G'day' to the guard and Brother Carey shook his hand and had a bit of a yarn.

Inside the gates everything was beautiful, the grass was the greenest I'd ever seen and there were flowers everywhere, and all different kinds of trees. It looked just like the pictures I'd seen of the big gardens in Sydney, that Mum was going to take me to one day.

We passed a couple of men in grey suits who were weeding a flower bed. They stood up

and waved and smiled at us but they didn't say anything.

'That's them,' said Ginge.

'They look alright to me,' I said.

Well, they did. I dunno what they were supposed to look like anyway. And now I could see that there were lots more of them, all gardening. Ginger suddenly pointed to between two trees.

'There's the cricket pitch.'

It was the flattest, greenest cricket pitch I'd ever seen.

We lost the toss, so we'd be fielding. I took my boots and socks off. I could run faster with bare feet.

A tall man was talking to two boys who were putting on pads. He was dressed in the grey suit of a patient.

'Who's that over there?'

'That's Henry,' Ginger said. 'Come over and meet him.'

'Will it be alright?'

'Yeah, of course it will. You'll like Henry.'

Ginger led me over to him.

'Henry, this is a new boy. Snowy Ball.'

'Hullo, Snowy. Welcome to Callan Park.'

'Thank you, Mr Henry.'

He roared with laughter. 'Just call me Henry,' he said.

Gee, the pitch was great to field on. The ground was so smooth and flat that the ball didn't bounce all over the place and the grass was so soft and green, I'll bet it was great to play footie on . . .

'Stop it, Snow, before it gets to the boundary.'

I ran as fast as I could after the ball but it was no good. I couldn't stop it.

'Four,' I yelled.

Suddenly, one of the patients got up from a bench, picked up the ball and ran off into the bushes with it. I didn't know what to do. I ran back onto the field.

'Did yer see that? He ran off with the ball.'

Everybody was laughing.

'Don't worry. That was Fred, he'll bring it back.'

Everyone sat or lay down on the grass and waited. They were right. After a few minutes, Fred came out of the bushes, walked right across the field to the wicketkeeper and gave him the ball.

'Thank you, Fred,' they all shouted.

Fred smiled and waved and walked back to his seat on the bench.

'Hey, Ginge, does he do that every time someone hits a four?'

'No, he just does it once and then if the ball goes near him again, he'll pick it up and throw it back on the field.'

What a funny thing to do. But I suppose that's why he was in here, because he did things like that.

'Ginge, which buildin' is the padded cell one?'

'That one at the end with all the barred windows. See that arm wavin' from the middle window? Well I've been comin' here for three years and that arm is always wavin'.'

For the rest of the match I couldn't take my eyes off that building. You could just make out some movement behind the bars, the shape of a face and another arm waving as we ran around on the green grass which they could see but would never walk on.

The days, weeks and months went by and I was getting on real good at school, making friends, not fighting, working at McIlwraith's the

grocery store on Saturdays, bottling Sunday mornings, collecting papers to sell to the fish shop, being picked for the footy team and playing a lot of our games at Birchgrove Oval, the home ground of the Balmain Tigers.

Mum had another baby girl. She was really beautiful and was called Philomena after the saint.

I remember all the family sitting around at night trying to decide what names to give the baby if it was a boy or if it was a girl. I never knew why parents went to so much trouble over names. Making out lists, asking people what they thought. With girls it was alright but with boys they all ended up with nicknames anyway—Chikka, Bluey, Ginger, Spanner, Nobby, Lofty, Shorty, Snowy, Spud. I suppose it was really to help when filling in forms and being christened. The priest couldn't say, 'I christen you "Spud Murphy". In the name of the Father and of the Son and of the Holy Ghost, Amen.' It just didn't sound right.

There were seven kids in our family now. Brian, me, Moya, Noni, Cletus, Joe and Phil. Dad wasn't earning much, I think it was about three pounds a week, and after paying rent, there

wasn't much left. Me and Brian gave all our money to Mum and she'd give us sixpence back for pocket money.

We'd all come home for lunch—most times having a running battle with the public school kids. Mum would make a pile of doughballs out of flour and water and then she'd fry them. They were like doughnuts only without the hole. They really filled you up.

I dunno how she did it but the food must've been alright because Brian and me played for our school in all the sports: football, tennis, swimming and athletics. The big athletics event of the year was on St Patrick's Day at the Sydney Sportsground, which all the Catholic schools entered, including the girls. I ran in the 100, 220 and the relay.

If you can imagine the Sydney Sportsground full of good Catholic boys and good Catholic girls all at the age when we were starting to get pimples and take a real interest in each other, you can understand why winning the 100, 220 and relay wasn't that important any more; well, not compared to getting a few addresses and exchanging school colours with the girls from some of the posh convent

schools, with the promise of 'I'll write and see you next year'.

One year, one of the boys from the under-14 relay team missed the race completely. He told the brother in charge that it wasn't his fault because four girls had tied him up under the main stand. It was such a far-fetched story I reckon he was telling the truth. The brother called him a liar—and anyway, what was he doing with four girls under the main stand in the first place? Golly, four girls? I reckon he wanted to be tied up . . . he'd be too strong for four girls, wouldn't he?

I came third in my class at the end of my first year in the high school, and the first four of us skipped second year and went straight into third year. I was now in the same class as Brian. We'd be doing our Intermediate together.

To begin with, I don't think he liked it very much, looking round and seeing his young brother sitting behind him. But Brian was my big brother, he'd always stick up for me, and had belted a few bullies over the years protecting me. I know he really didn't mind. He might've even been proud of me.

I found third year pretty hard. I seemed to

spend so much time playing sport for the school, coaching the younger kids and working that I didn't have much time for studying. It was during that year that a priest came around and had a chat with the boys in our class about a vocation, asking if any of us wanted to be a priest or a brother. When he spoke to me, I said I wouldn't mind being a sports brother, you know, just teaching sport. He said he'd pray for me and would I do the same for him. Why did they always say that?

That idea didn't last very long because I found I was thinking more about girls than I was about God, and I don't think *that* was the right way to go about getting what the priest called 'a real vocation'. I am now thinking about girls more than ever after a girl from Rozelle Convent, who I'd been winking at, pulled me into the changing sheds at Elkington Park baths and kissed me right on the lips, just like they do in the movies. It was real good. I really liked it.

I gave up the brotherhood and went back to wanting to be a cowboy on the films.

'Hey, Snow. Chikka can do it!'

'Are yer jokin'? He's not old enough.'

'He said it happened last night.'

'Where is he?'

'Over there.'

Ginger pointed to a small group of boys who seemed to be hanging on the every word of a tall, fair wavy-haired boy of about thirteen and a half. He was Chikka Evans, holder of the Junior Cup for athletics and the fastest runner for his age in the school.

'Chikka, is it true?'

'Yeah, Snow. It happened last night. I was ... er ... sort of muckin' around in the ... er ... bath and it just sort of happened.'

'What was it like?'

'Well, Snow. Ah ... it was like er ... I dunno ... er ... sorta funny ... real good ... it ... ah ...'

'I read in a book that it was like "a flock of eagles flyin' outa yer arse". Is that true Chikka?'

'A flock of eagles? No, how could a flock of ... ah yer kiddin'.'

'Yer not havin' us on, are yer?'

'No, honest.'

The rest of the crowd started muttering to themselves—'big skite', 'liar', 'bullshit'.

'Alright. If you think I'm lyin', I'll prove it

to you after school. The bet's two bob. We'll go down to the gravel pit.'

'Okay Chikka, we'll be there.'

Between the lot of us we raked up the two bob.

The gravel pit was an almost perfect circle, a bit bigger than a boxing ring and about four feet deep. It looked like a small arena. And it was, in a way, because most of the fights in our school took place there. The two fighters would get down into the pit while the urgers yelled advice from the top. It often reminded me of those pictures of gladiators fighting in the Roman times.

After school we all split up into twos and threes, otherwise one of the bro's might get a bit suspicious if he saw a group of twenty boys heading for the gravel pit. It took about fifteen minutes to walk there. You had to cross all the railway lines of the shunting yards just behind the wheat silos at White Bay.

'Are yer ready, Chikka?' someone asked.

'Yeah.'

But he wasn't. He looked a bit shy and he couldn't turn his back on us because he was in the middle of a circle of boys. None of us looked

very happy either. Finally, he got going.

The twenty-odd boys shuffled about and most of them looked away. A couple started talking about trains, some were whistling, hardly anyone was watching him, except every now and then we'd have a quick look to see how he was doing. I looked at the railway trucks with country names on them, full of wheat that would be stored in the silos and then shipped to other countries.

'Hurry up, Chikka. I gotta get home,' someone said.

'I'm goin' as fast as I can!'

And he was too. His face looked like a beet-root. I'll bet it was hot down in that pit.

Most of the fellers were losing interest by now, some were throwing stones at an old kero tin, some were just staring up at the sky.

'Chikka's masturbatin',' said Egghead.

'What? Chikka's masturbatin'? No,' I said. 'Yer wrong 'cos me mum said that we should masturbate our food twenty-four times, 'cos it was good for our digestion.'

'No,' said Egghead. 'I'll bet your mum said "masticate". Masturbating is wanking and mas-ticating is chewing.'

'Honest?'

'Yeah, honest.'

I reckon he was right because Egghead was top of the class and was always using big words.

'It's comin' now,' yelled Chikka.

Twenty heads swung round as we all sort of froze in our tracks. Chikka opened his eyes wide and gave a little shiver.

We waited for a bit but nothing else happened. Chikka just did up his fly.

'Is that all, Chikka?'

'Yeah. That's all.'

'Strewth. What a waste of bloody time,' someone yelled.

Everybody shot off in different directions. The last I heard as I ran across the tracks was Chikka yelling, 'What about me two bob?'

What about his two bob? What about all that stuff in the pictures, when the girl and the man would be kissing and they lay back on the grass or fell onto the bed? Quickly the screen would be filled with fireworks bursting, or waves crashing on the rocks or guns going off or a roll of drums. And in some books I'd read, there was a 'roaring in the ears' and 'floating above the

clouds' and the one I liked best, 'and the earth moved'.

But just a little shiver?

'Why are you so late home from school, Vince?' asked Mum.

'Ah, I . . . er . . . was muckin' around in class and . . . er . . . I . . . er . . . was kept back to clean up the playground.'

Three weeks later I won the Junior Cup for athletics. Chikka came second. Somebody said he lost because he had 'wanker's doom'. You know, doing it all the time—they reckon it weakens you.

Mum was really working hard. Cooking, cleaning and washing by hand for nine people. She said she missed having a decent yard to hang up the clothes and maybe grow some flowers and vegetables or even keep a few chooks.

Dad asked the PMG if he could be shifted somewhere out of Rozelle. He asked to be sent to a depot at Epping. He'd been there a couple of times and said it was a real nice place, with trees and parks and tennis courts and you could go for walks in the bush. But it would cost a lot more to rent a house there and he didn't think

he could pay it on what he was earning.

So it was worked out that if he got the job at Epping and Brian and me got our Intermediate Certificates, Brian would leave school and get a job to help keep the family and I would stay on at school until I was old enough to leave. It also meant I'd have to go to a new school, Burwood Christian Brothers. After Rozelle I didn't want to start at another school, I just wanted to get a job and start earning.

Everything happened in six weeks. Dad got the job at Epping. We found a nice little house in Melrose Street, number 16. It had three bed-rooms, a living room, kitchen, bathroom, outside dunny and a back verandah big enough for all of us boys to sleep on. Brian and me passed our Intermediate and Brian got a job.

Even with Brian working, Mum and Dad didn't seem to have enough money to keep us because a couple of times I went over to Lakemba to see Mum's brother, my Uncle Pat, and collect an envelope for her. I reckon there was money in it.

'Mum, are you borrowin' money off Uncle Pat?'

She didn't answer for a bit but she had that

worried look on her face that I'd seen a lot lately. Things must be real crook to get Mum down. She didn't laugh as much as she used to and that seemed to affect the whole family.

'We're behind with the rent. Your Uncle Pat has lent us the money to pay it.'

'Mum, I gotta leave school and get a job. Yer can't keep borrowin' off Uncle Pat. And anyway, I don't like Burwood Brothers much. Not after Rozelle.'

She ruffled my hair and said, 'We'll see. Go on now or you'll be late for school. We'll talk about it tonight. Your footie shorts are on the line.'

And she quickly walked away.

There was the usual flutter of butterflies in my gut as I trotted out with the rest of the team to play my first game for Burwood Christian Brothers.

Aw strewth. I'd been marking him for three years, all the time I was at Rozelle, and now there he was again—that big inside centre from Manly Christian Brothers, looking bigger than ever. I was always hoping he'd outgrow his strength but he never did.

You could say we were on nodding terms

because that's all we'd ever done. Nodded. Never talked or said 'G'day'. Just nodded to each other ... y'know, at that moment when you're sizing each other up; when both teams are facing each other just before the kick-off.

You could hear the crack all over Concord oval as a Manly player tackled me from behind. I didn't feel any pain at first, I just kept looking at this strange left arm in front of me. From the elbow down it was pointing in the wrong direction.

'Tough luck, mate,' said the big Manly inside centre and touched me on the shoulder.

'The ambulance is on its way, Snow.'

I had a feeling that my schooldays were over. I was fourteen.

four

RABBITING WITH MARY

I WAS STILL IN SHORT pants when I started my first job at Stoddard's Millinery Warehouse in Clarence Street, delivering hats to the posh ladies' hat shops around Sydney. They called them 'salons'.

All that people saw of me was a stack of big, round hatboxes, with a couple of legs underneath walking quickly or running to make up time, because the boxes were so big I couldn't get on the trams. I needed a lot of room and the conductors were always telling me to 'try the one behind. It's pretty empty'. It hardly ever was.

My wages were thirteen and nine pence a week and I'd been working there for a couple of months, until one Saturday morning the boss complained that I was behind with my deliveries. I was too, because a couple of rush orders had come in and had to be delivered straightaway. I

tried to explain to him that I'd been flat out since eight o'clock. I'd worked pretty hard ever since I started with them but there was just too much for me to do and they wouldn't get any more help. They expected me to do the lot. My boss began to yell and shout and said I was bloody lazy.

I think it was the 'bloody lazy' that did it and it took all the guts I had to stand up to him and say, 'Yer can stick yer fur felts, yer panamas, yer boxes and yer job up yer arse.'

And I took off out the front door, thinking as I was doing it that I'd just lost a day and a half's pay.

McMaster Holland Solicitors—I was their new office boy. I'd left Stoddard's on the Saturday and had started my new job on the Tuesday. I'd only been one day out of work.

It wasn't a bad sort of job; running messages, doing the mail and taking legal documents to the courthouse and the Registrar General. I felt pretty important. Besides, I was wearing my first pair of long 'uns. Mum had put a pair on lay-by when I was at the millinery warehouse. It felt strange at first having my legs all covered up.

Roy Rene—'Mo'—was one of our clients

and when he came in to see Mr Holland, he'd always say 'G'day' to me as he passed. He was a friendly sort of bloke.

Mr McMaster called me in one day and asked me if I'd like to become an articled clerk with the hopes of becoming a solicitor or even a barrister in the future. He showed me some of the books that I'd have to study at night school. They were huge and the print was so small that they frightened the life out of me.

I said, 'No, because one day pretty soon I'd be goin' to America.'

I didn't tell him why. I knew that I'd be doing my fighting on horseback with six-guns in front of cameras and not in the law courts.

Mr McMaster said that there was no point in me staying if I didn't want to become a solicitor, all I'd ever be was an office boy.

I said I'd look for another job and gave him a week's notice. McMaster Holland were pretty good to me, giving me time off for job interviews and not docking my pay.

I am now the new office boy for the Australian General Electric at Auburn and twice a day I take the mail from there to the head office in Kent Street.

I don't know how many magazines of *Ranch Romances* I'd read on the train journeys from Auburn to Town Hall. Must've been hundreds. There were about six or seven stories in each magazine. All about the West—about beautiful girls, fine horses and lean-hipped, hard-muscled cowboys who were so fast on the draw that their hands were just a blur. That's what I wanted to be on the films, but how was I ever going to get to Hollywood? I was already fifteen and only earnin' seventeen and ninepence a week.

My first ever holiday and it was to be in the bush. What could be better? Two weeks' holiday after working a year at AGE. It was Mum's idea.

'You've never had a holiday away from home and Aunty Kit would love to have you on the farm.'

Uncle Nick picked me up at Molong railway station in an old ute truck.

'It's about eight miles to the property,' he said. 'Aunty Kit's lookin' forward to seein' you again.'

Gum trees, galahs, rabbits, crows—I could see them all as the ute roared along the dirt road.

Just like Moree. I kept looking at the bush, remembering what it was like five years ago.

Aunty Kit made a great fuss of me.

'Tea will be ready in half an hour—a baked dinner.'

'All off the farm,' said Uncle Nick. 'Mutton, potatoes, pumpkin, cabbage, even the apples for the apple pie.'

It was a great meal.

'I hear you're a bit of a milker, so you can look after the two cows we've got,' said Uncle Nick. 'I'll get you up in time.'

And he did.

I hadn't forgotten how to milk and before long I was into a nice rhythm, my head resting on the side of the cow and she was letting her milk down which meant she was relaxed.

All that Uncle Nick said when I showed him the amount of milk I'd got was, 'Not bad.'

I must be hearing things—I'd just taken a couple of mouthfuls of porridge when I'm sure Uncle Nick farted. Aunty Kit didn't say anything or even look up so I thought I must have been imagining it. I mean, nobody would fart on purpose while you're eating your breakfast. No, I'm not

hearing things! Uncle Nick let go another ripper and didn't even stop eating.

'Aw Nick! Not at the table,' said Aunty Kit.

'It's best to fart and stink a little than break yer arse and be a cripple,' was all he said between mouthfuls.

Didn't even say sorry or pardon.

'We're goin' visitin' this afternoon over to the Evans' place, it's about an hour's ride in the sulky. Yer Aunty likes to get out of the house for a bit on Sundays.'

It was really good, the three of us sitting there, clip-clopping along the bush road. Aunty Kit with her sunshade, Uncle Nick puffing on his pipe. It took me back all those years ago, to Wee Waa. Mum, Dad, Brian, me, Moya and Noni driving in the sulky every Sunday afternoon.

The Evans were nice country people, and they had a daughter, Mary, who was twenty-four. She'd tried working in Sydney but she didn't like it so had come back to work on the farm. Said she preferred country life.

'And don't call me "Miss". I'm not that old!'

Just as we were leaving, she asked me if I would like to go rabbiting.

'I'll ride over. We'll take a rifle and a couple of dogs. That's if it's okay with your Uncle Nick.'

Uncle Nick, who was standing nearby, said, 'Yeah, sure. No worries.'

Mary arrived about ten the next morning carrying a rifle, riding a nice chestnut mare and with a couple of kangaroo dogs. Aunty Kit had packed some lunch and a bottle of homemade lemon drink into the saddlebag and Uncle Nick let me take the .22 rifle and half a box of .22 longs.

I suppose we'd been hunting for about an hour. Well 'hunting' really was the wrong word, there were so many bloody rabbits about that you didn't really have to move. Just like Moree—thousands of them. You just sat in one spot and shot them, even the dogs got fed up after a while. We had six already, which was enough.

'We'll gut 'em and then let's go over to the dam and have lunch and get out of the sun for a bit,' Mary said.

The dam, which was a pretty fair size, was fed by a windmill. Four large trees grew near the water's edge. We unsaddled the horses, let them

have a drink, then put them in the shade and slung the rabbits up into the fork of one of the trees to stop the ants from crawling all over them.

'Spread your saddle blanket out, makes the ground softer,' Mary said.

Lying there looking up at the branches of the gum tree, the blue sky, listening to the calls of the birds, the horses tearing at the grass, and all the other sounds of the bush. Gee, I missed this in the city.

'Let's go for a swim,' said Mary.

'I ... er ... didn't bring a cossie.'

'Who needs a cossie,' she said, pulling off her boots and socks. She started to unbutton her shirt—very slowly I thought. She was taking her time; one button, two buttons, three buttons, four buttons. Then she pulled her shirt out of her trousers, took it off and threw it at me.

It landed on my face and I could smell scent on it.

She stood there in her trousers and brassiere only about three feet away.

'Come on. Don't be shy.'

She unbuckled her belt and started to undo the buttons on each side of her trousers, then

Mum and Dad on their wedding day.

Dad, Moya, Brian, me, Mum and Noni in Moree.

My brothers and sisters (Philomena is missing) in 1991.
LEFT TO RIGHT: Cletus, me, Noni, Brian, Moya, Joe.

ABOVE: Nodding off.
Me and Brian in Wee Waa.

LEFT: Who's for tennis?
Me and Brian in Wee Waa.

Off to work. My first job. I was fourteen.

Off to fight the Hun,
World War Two.

The Old Digger.
Me, Anzac Day, 1993.

Wireless training in Canada.
That's me at the back.

'Jonesy', Owen Jones.
Edinburgh, 1994.

The infamous 547 Squadron rugby team.
Me: back row, far left. Johnny Day: second row, centre.

The Holy Hour on
O'Connell Street,
Dublin 1944.

Drama students in
Sydney, 1946. Bill
Redmond, Doreen
and me.

pushed them down to her ankles and kicked them off.

I couldn't take my eyes off her.

She then reached around behind her back, unhooked something and took off her brassiere. Then she pushed her bloomers down and stepped out of them. She stood in front of me, naked, just looking at me.

I'd never seen a woman naked all over before. The hair round her private parts was black and curly and her breasts looked firm and they sort of stuck out and up.

I could feel something crawling up my leg. I'd been in such a dream watching Mary take her clothes off that I hadn't seen my blanket was covered in bull ants. They were everywhere, attracted by the horse sweat in the blanket, I suppose, and now they were having a go at me.

'Bloody hell!'

A sudden sharp pain had me jumping up and down, slapping my legs and rubbing where they were biting.

'Get your clothes off quick and get into the water. It's the only way to get rid of them,' yelled Mary.

I didn't have to be told twice. I was already

ripping my trousers off and it was only when I was in the water and the biting had stopped that I remembered that Mary was naked—and so was I—and we were swimming together.

We swam round a bit, raced each other across the dam, splashed each other. The water was fairly muddy so we couldn't see our naked bodies.

'I'm going to dry off,' said Mary.

I watched her walk slowly out of the dam and stand in the sun slowly rubbing the water off her body with her hands. She always seemed to do things in slow motion.

'Aren't you coming out?'

'Yeah, I'm on my way,' I said. Not moving.

She looked really nice, her whole body shining from the water. She stood there rubbing her hands all over herself and just looking at me.

How was I going to get out of the water without her seeing me? I'd never been naked in front of a woman before.

Aw, no ... Crikey ... Strewth! I was start-ing to get a horn.

I turned around and swam flat out across the dam and back again, thinking of football,

tennis, anything. That did the trick because it went down.

I plucked up courage, raced out towards my clothes, trying not to look at Mary, who was lying on her blanket. But I couldn't help myself. My eyes kept going back to that patch of black curly hair.

I turned away and rubbed the water off me, looking at the horses and dogs.

They just looked back. Wondering, I suppose, what we were up to. I was scared and shy as I turned to get my trousers. I shook them out and hurried away from the bull-ants' nest.

'Don't put your clothes on yet. Lie down for a bit.'

I didn't lie down. I sat hunched up with my knees under my chin and my arms round my legs, sort of hiding everything, looking at the dam.

'Have you ever touched a woman's breast before?'

'No.'

'Would you like to?'

'Ah ... well, er ... yeah ... I er ... er ... wouldn't mind.'

'Put your left hand on my right breast.'

'I'm right-handed,' I said. 'Does that matter?'

'Just do what I tell you.'

I put my left hand on her right breast.

'Now put your other hand down there.'

'What? Down there?'

'Yes, down there.'

'Down there?'

'Yes, down there! It won't bite.'

I put my other hand down there . . . Crikey.

'Now gently squeeze my breast with your left hand and rub . . . down there . . . with your right hand.'

By this time I was getting in a bit of a state because it was like trying to, you know, pat your head and rub your tummy at the same time. I couldn't get it right to start with. I was squeezing when I should've been rubbing and rubbing when I should've been squeezing or both hands were either squeezing or rubbing.

I'd forgotten about anything else because I was trying so hard to get my hands to do what they were supposed to do and at the same time brushing away the bull ants that we were attracting.

Squeeze with the left, rub with the right.

Squeeze with the left, rub with the right.

It was a bit like the dancing lessons I used to have.

Two steps to the left and one to the right.

Two steps to the left and one to the right.

Now one to the right and two to the left.

Now one to the right and two to the left.

Suddenly Mary let out a yell. It sounded like '*Ow!*'

'Have yer been bitten?'

'No, I haven't been bitten,' she sort of gasped.

By now the dogs were on their feet thinking they were going home, the horses had stopped feeding and the galahs in the next tree took off in a great flutter of wings and squawks.

I'd never seen anything like it and this was only one person doing it, whatever it was, and all by herself too. Golly, what would it be like if two people were doing it?

'We've got to get some French letters,' she said. 'So that we can do it properly. I'll give you some money. Go into Molong to the chemist and you get a packet of Durex. Will you do that?'

'Yeah. Right,' I said without thinking.

Like they said in those western stories—I

rode tall in the saddle and felt different on the way back. Real grown up. I'd made love to a woman, well, sort of. And now I had five shillings in my pocket to buy some French letters for the day after tomorrow.

I'd been hanging round the chemist shop for about half an hour. I didn't have the guts to go in and ask the woman serving behind the counter for French letters. I was hoping the man working up under the sign 'Prescriptions' would come down and serve or maybe the woman would go to lunch or something.

I'd never bought French letters before. I'd only ever seen one once. We found it near the tennis courts in Moree and tied it to a tap to see how much water it'd hold before bursting. It filled up like a large balloon, bigger than a football before it burst. They really are made of strong rubber.

The man was serving behind the counter and the woman was nowhere in sight. Now's my chance ... Here goes.

I walked into the shop trying to look as old as I could. I was wearing one of Uncle Nick's felt hats, I thought it might help.

'Yes, young man? What can I do for you?'
he asked.

While I was plucking up courage, the
bloody phone started ringing from the prescriptions counter.

'Oh, excuse me,' he said. 'I'll just answer
that. It might be an emergency.' And he headed
for the phone.

'Can I help you?'

It was that woman. She appeared out of
nowhere.

'Er . . . yes,' I said. I could feel my face going
red. 'I want some . . . er . . . toothpaste.'

'What brand?'

'Er . . . Ipana.'

'Large or small?'

'Small.'

'Anything else?' There seemed to be a bit of
a smile on her face.

'No, thanks. Just the toothpaste.'

Doesn't she *ever* eat? I was still hanging
around outside the chemist's waiting for her to
go to lunch.

I think she caught sight of me a couple of
times.

The man was at last behind the counter—

the woman was nowhere to be seen and the shop was empty.

This is it!

I'd taken about four steps into the shop: 'Did you forget something?' ... and there she was, filling one of the shelves. 'It's alright, Mr Wheeler. I'll serve the young lad. You go to lunch. Now, what did you forget?'

'Er ... razor blades.'

'Razor blades?' she looked at my face which was pretty red by now. 'What kind of razor blades does your father, uncle or older brother want?' she asked. 'Folding razor or safety?'

'Safety.'

'Gem or Gillette?'

'Er ... Gem.' I know she knew what I really wanted. If I'd said 'some Durex', she would probably have said, 'How many packets?' But I didn't have the guts.

What would Mary say? I hadn't been able to think of anything else except the next time we'd be at the dam. And now I wouldn't be able to do it properly.

Mary arrived the following day driving a ute.

'I won't be coming rabbiting today,' she said. 'Did you get the ... you know?'

'No. I didn't have the guts. There was a woman servin' in the shop.'

'What did you end up with?'

'Gem razor blades and Ipana toothpaste.'

Mary roared with laughter. 'Razor blades and toothpaste! I'll see you in about four days,' and she took off in a cloud of dust.

Strike a light! Four days.

'I'll be goin' to the market tomorrow,' said Uncle Nick. 'I want to buy a ram and I hear there's one goin' cheap 'cos he's only got one ball ... but that shouldn't make a great deal of difference,' he said thoughtfully.

We went to the market and bought the ram with one ball. Well, he may have only had one but Uncle Nick said by the look and feel of it, it was a big 'un.

'I want you to watch him for a couple of hours to see how he works.'

I saddled up the horse, took a bit of food and followed Uncle Nick in the ute with the ram to one of the paddocks that held a large mob of sheep. The ram was let out, Uncle Nick went back to the house and I sat under a tree and watched and waited.

That ram didn't even bother to eat any grass but headed straight for the sheep.

Talk about a good buy—he never stopped! And he was so quick, he couldn't have had time to enjoy it.

Uncle Nick had put some sort of red dye on his chest and underbelly so that he could tell which ewe the ram had had a go at. By the time I left, the whole flock seemed to have a reddish haze over their backs.

'He's workin' real well, Uncle Nick. I don't think he could have done any better with two balls. You'll see in the mornin'.'

Never mind the bloody ram, all I could think about was Mary and watching that ram in action didn't help.

The next four days went pretty slowly. I was still milking the cows and working hard around the farm and Uncle Nick was still farting at the table.

And then, there she was, Mary on her chestnut mare with rifle and dogs.

'Well, are you ready to go rabbiting?'

Gee, was I ready to go rabbiting!

The rest of the holiday went by in a sort of dream.

Mary was a great teacher. Well, I think she was because I didn't have anybody to compare her with, but whatever she was teaching me, I was liking. Though it would've been even better if the ground wasn't so hard and those bloody bull ants hadn't always been around, and if we hadn't had to keep remembering to fire off a few shots now and then so Uncle Nick would think we were rabbiting.

After about five days of trying to do it twice a day, I was just about starting to get the hang of it.

'Take your time,' Mary kept saying. 'Take your time. Don't be in such a hurry.'

Well, I was always in a bit of a hurry at the end of it . . . you know . . . when . . . er . . . and also when it was time to go back because we had to shoot about six rabbits so Uncle Nick wouldn't get suspicious. To return without any rabbits after a day's rabbiting in the bush where there were millions would really make him wonder.

The holiday came to an end and it was time to say goodbye.

'Mary, mightn't yer have a baby?' I asked.

'No, it's alright. Don't worry. Let's hope the "rhythm" system works.'

'The "rhythm" system, what's that?'

'Don't you worry about it, it'll be alright.'

'I'll never forget you, Mary. I just wish I was a bit older.'

'Yes, so do I,' she said, smiling.

'You're sure yer won't have a baby?'

'Yes, I'm sure. If you don't hear from me in the next four weeks, you'll know everything's alright.'

Aunty Kit and Uncle Nick saw me off at the station.

What a great holiday!

I remember reading in a book somewhere a saying: 'He went away a boy and came back a man.' Well, maybe not a man but I could be a father and I was only fifteen. A father at fifteen and earnin' seventeen and nine a week. Bloody hell!

'When did you last go to confession, Vince?'

I'd been dreading that question ever since I got back from Uncle Nick's.

'Aw, a few weeks ago, Mum.'

'Well, I want the whole family to go to communion this Sunday—it's Palm Sunday. You'll have time to go to confession before you go to the pictures on Saturday.'

I never minded going to confession before because there was never much to confess, just 'bad thoughts' and a few other things that boys my age did. And when you said, 'I've had bad thoughts, Father,' he never asked you, 'Bad thoughts about what?' He seemed to know. But this one was going to be different.

I'd *done* the 'bad thoughts', and I'd have to tell him about Mary. And I'd have to tell him the truth because I was in a state of mortal sin, which I didn't like, being a Catholic and all that. Anyway, you'd have to make an act of perfect contrition, promising you'd never commit those sins again. Well, not till you're married. That seemed an awful long time. Even if I got married when I was twenty-five that'd mean I'd have to wait another ten years. I knew in the back of my mind that I wouldn't be able to last that long because I liked it.

I blessed myself, 'In the name of the Father and of the Son and of the Holy Ghost. Amen.'

'How long is it since your last confession?'

'Three weeks, Father,' I was trying to make my voice sound deeper.

'Have you anything to confess, my son?'

'Yes, Father ... er ...'

I couldn't go on. I'd gone over it in my mind a hundred times. I'd looked up the right words in the dictionary and everything.

The soft, kindly voice of the priest said, 'Don't be afraid, my son. God is all forgiving. What is it you want to confess?'

I had to get it over with or we'd be here all night and the John Wayne picture started at 7.30 and I bet there'd be a lot of penance to say.

'I've had sexual intercourse ten times since my last confession, Father.'

I don't know whether I blurted it out too loudly or what but everything went very quiet, a sort of hush came over the whole church or I thought it did and there was some movement behind the little window. I think the priest was trying to see who it was but I moved my head back and pressed the side of my face up against the wall so he couldn't see me. Anyway, I don't think they're supposed to see you when you're confessing.

'How old are you, my son?'

His voice now seemed different. It wasn't as soft and friendly as it was before.

'Fifteen, Father.'

'*Fifteen*?'

'Yes, Father.'

'You know what you have done is a mortal sin?'

'Yes, Father.'

'*Ten* mortal sins.'

'Yes, Father.'

I'd been hoping that it'd be just one pretty big one, but *ten*! I'd be here all night saying penance. I'd never done *ten* in one go before; I could feel the weight of them pressing down on me.

'Did you take precautions?' He wasn't saying 'my son' any more.

'Precautions, Father?'

'Yes ... er ... did you ... er ... practise birth control ... er ... did you wear anything?'

'No, Father. We were both naked.'

There was another long silence and he sort of sighed in the middle of it.

'You must promise me you will not see this girl again and, what's more important, you must promise *God* that you will avoid all temptation and never see her again.'

'Yes, Father.'

'Now I want you to make an act of perfect contrition.'

The John Wayne picture had started when I got there. The fellers had kept a seat for me.

'You were a long time, Snow. Did you have a lot of "bad thoughts" to confess?'

'Very funny. There was a crowd of people in front of me.'

Before the priest gave me absolution, he'd said, 'And for your penance I want you to say the Rosary, before you leave the church.'

I knew why he'd said 'before you leave the church', he knew that most of the young blokes said their penance in the street on the way to the pictures.

No wonder I was late.

The next four weeks were a nightmare. I couldn't think straight. Mum thought I was coming down with something.

'And you looked so well when you came back. You said you'd put on five pounds.'

How do you tell your family that you could be a father? And that all your brothers and sisters would be the youngest aunts and uncles in Epping?

'There's a letter from Molong,' said Mum.

My heart stopped beating.

'Oh, yeah?' Trying to be casual.

'It's from Aunty Kit, saying how much they liked having you and that Mary Evans sends her regards and says she's fit and well and hopes you're the same. Isn't that nice of her?'

FIVE

DANCING WITH
DEANNA DURBIN

I DUNNO WHAT IT IS, but everybody wants to educate me. I was called into the secretary's office, Mr Dean, and offered a correspondence course in accountancy with Blennerhassetts. All I had to do was pass the exams and AGE would pay the fees. They hoped that when I became an accountant I would continue to work for them.

I talked it over with Mum and Dad and they thought it was a pretty good idea; said it was a great opportunity to get on.

I didn't want to get on. I wanted to go to Hollywood. But Mum was so keen, and I dunno, I didn't want to hurt her. So I started the course, studied quite hard and by the time I was seventeen I was in charge of the bonus department, responsible for bonus payments to most of the workers in the factory.

By this time all hell had broken loose in

Europe and we were at war with Germany and Italy. The AIF were fighting in the Middle East and England was fighting for its life against that madman Hitler.

Part of our factory had been turned over to making guns, twenty-five pounders, and AGE was classed as a protected industry, which meant you couldn't leave your job. Three weeks before my eighteenth birthday I told Mr Sanders, my boss, that when I was eighteen I was going to join the RAAF. I wanted to be a fighter pilot. He said I was in a 'protected industry' and couldn't join up.

'Mr Sanders, on my eighteenth birthday I will stop work and just sit here until you let me go. Anyway, it'd be a few months before I would be actually called up, plenty of time to train somebody else.'

The Japs attacked Pearl Harbor on 7 December 1941, three days after my eighteenth birthday. We were now fighting the Japs as well. So I went away to the war. Just like big brother Brian who was in the Army.

Not as a fighter pilot as I had hoped, but as a wireless air gunner. I put it all down to my interview with the Wing Commander on the

selection board at Bradfield Park, who happened to see me play Rugby during the week.

'Ball, I felt you played a rather selfish game on Wednesday. In the second half you practically ignored your outside-centre and I thought you held onto the ball too much.'

'Sir, every time I passed to him, he either dropped it, kicked it, knocked it on, fell over or if he did manage to hold onto the ball, he didn't know what to do with it. That's why I had to go myself sometimes.'

'Ball, in the Air Force team spirit is what counts. Individuality is all very well but you have to help and give support when and where it is needed.'

'Sir, we wanted to win that game and the only way we were gunna' do that was to get it out to our wingers, who were good. And sir, we did win in the end by two points. And I did score two tries.'

'Thank you, Ball. I was well aware you scored two tries. You didn't have to tell me.'

The way he said that, made it sound like I was skiting.

Aw shit! There it was on the noticeboard. The results of the Selection Board.

422376 LAC Ball V.M. Wireless Air Gunner.

I felt sick. It kicked the arse right out of my world. So much for being a fighter pilot.

After that I really didn't give a stuff. I got drunk that night with Owen Jones and Bruce Burton and was sick all over the table in a crowded restaurant above Wynyard station. Jonesy reckons I cleared the place in five minutes flat.

They made that outside centre a trainee pilot. I often wondered if he got his wings and if he did, whether he was a better pilot than he was an outside centre. Who knows, he might have made a great pilot.

Our postings were up on the board. Jonesy and me would be going to Canada to start our training as WAGs and Bruce would be staying in Australia as a trainee pilot. Would miss Bruce. Lucky bugger, being a pilot.

Saying goodbye to Mum, Dad and the family was pretty hard. I tried to be cheerful and kept saying I'd be alright and not to worry and, anyway, by the time I finished training the war would probably be over. Mum kissed me on both cheeks and whispered, 'Look after yourself and don't forget to say your prayers.' Dad shook

my hand hard and said, 'Good luck.' He put his arm around Mum and took her inside. In a rush I said goodbye to Moya, Noni, Clete, Joe and Phil, grabbed my kitbag and ran down the front steps before I started bawling.

As we sailed through the Heads the ship's rails were crowded with trainee air crew soaking up the last glimpses of the Sydney coastline, not knowing how long it would be before we saw it again. Without any doubt though, I always knew that I would be coming back. The thought of getting killed had never occurred to me. Well, that's not true really. I'd been thinking a lot about Nora Nell lately and what she'd look like now after about seven years and if I got killed I'd never see her again. And I had promised to come back for her one day. She'd be eighteen now, my age, and maybe she'd grown tired of waiting and had a boyfriend or was even married. I had to find out, so I wrote to her old address in Moree, saying that I'd joined up and was going overseas and would like to write to her, and could I have a photo.

The letter must have got lost in the post or she had moved because I didn't receive an

answer. I'd have liked to have had a picture of Nora Nell to take with me.

The USS *Mount Vernon*, a converted passenger liner, was taking us to San Francisco. From there we'd go to Edmonton, Canada, and then on to Calgary for our wireless training.

Two days out of Sydney, we had a *short arm* parade. We were all lined up on deck waiting for the inspection. Then the doc arrived. Strewth, a *lady* doctor.

We were all pretty young and shy about having a *lady* doctor inspect our privates.

'Pull the foreskin back. Cough. Cough.' And so she went on down the line.

Wait till she gets to Chalky White! We reckoned that he'd grown on *it*—not the other way around. I still say she stood longer in front of Chalky than anyone else. And Jonesy reckoned her eyes opened just a little bit wider.

Jonesy and me missed the train from Frisco, due to the great hospitality of the Yanks and with the help of the US Army, arrived three days late in Edmonton.

'Just one person does the talkin',' Jonesy said. 'You.'

We got off pretty easy. 'Don't let that happen again,' was all they said.

Thinking about it afterwards, I wondered how they could believe all those white lies I told them. Maybe they didn't. They just let us off anyway.

'Aw come on Jonesy, you must be able to do it, it's so bloody easy.'

'I dunno Snow, I must have a mental block where morse code is concerned. Anyway if I fail this exam they're gunna' make me a straight gunner.'

Aw crikey. Jonesy was one of my best mates. We'd played junior football for Eastwood together, joined up together and when the Selection Board had made him a trainee observer, he'd asked to be changed over to a wireless air gunner so he could go to Canada with me.

Jonesy failed the morse code exam and was posted to a gunnery school.

The night before he left, about eight of us decided that there should be a proper send-off for our old mate and headed for the pubs of Calgary, where we drank large amounts of booze, became maudlin and tearful, and said

we'd write lots of letters and meet up in England fighting the Hun or in the Pacific fighting the Japs.

As we staggered up the hill towards camp, slipping and sliding all over the place, Siddy Hill, another good mate and the most sober amongst us, pointed to a black object lying in the snow by the side of the road. We stumbled over to have a look.

'Shit.' It was Robbo, who'd been with us earlier until he'd been sick and said he couldn't take any more so he had headed back to camp. The poor bugger was as stiff as a board; we thought he was dead. Somehow we managed to get him to our hut, carrying him like a plank of wood. We took off his clothes and put him under a hot shower and a couple of us rubbed him with hot towels. Somebody had already gone for the doc.

'I don't know what he's been drinking,' said the doc, 'but the high alcohol content in his bloodstream saved his life. And that was good thinking, putting him under the hot shower.'

I suppose poor Robbo, still feeling pretty crook, thought he'd have a bit of a spell halfway up the hill, sat down and just passed out. Thank

God he'd been downing his favourite drink—whisky with a beer chaser.

We're always reading about the evils of drink. Well this was one time the evils of drink did some good.

Jonesy left the next day, looking terrible.

'See you in England, Snow.'

'Yeah, see you in England. We'll keep in touch. Luck.'

I missed having Jonesy around. But there were exams to pass and new skills to learn. So far the war had been like one long holiday: skiing every weekend at Banff in the Rockies; being taught to ice-skate by friendly Canadian girls, invited to their homes; parties, pubs, pumpkin pie, flapjacks and maple syrup.

'What are we gunna' do on our fortnight's leave?'

Siddy Hill, Johnny Day, Nigel Moon and me were on our fifth beer and we still couldn't make up our minds.

'This may sound a little crazy,' I said. 'But why don't we hitchhike to Hollywood?'

'Crazy? Right, Snow. Yer bloody mad! Do yer know where Hollywood is? And *hitchhike*,

it's bloody winter!' So, on and on they went.

New ideas were suggested, thrown out and the beer kept flowing. I think it was around about the tenth beer that Siddy said, 'Yer know that Hollywood idea of Snow's isn't bad. Well it would be different, wouldn't it? It can't be any worse than gettin' an ack-ack shell up yer arse.'

Which we all knew eventually would be on the cards.

'Yeah, why don't we give it a go?' I said.

'I'm game,' said Syd.

'Nig?'

'Johnny?'

Four glazed looks and nods all round.

'Okay.' 'Okay.' 'Okay.' 'Okay.'

'Let's shake on it,' I said. Once you shook on it, there was no way of getting out of it.

The next two weeks just flew by. All I could think about was Hollywood; of going to the place where they made all those westerns. All my dreams of being a cowboy on the films came back to me; of my boyhood heros—Buck Jones, Tom Mix, Tim McCoy, Hoot Gibson. Maybe we'd meet some of the stars.

We caught a bus from Calgary to Cranbrook, which was not far from the US border,

and with the help of the locals were directed to the main road heading south out of town towards the USA.

I reckon it took all of five minutes to get our first lift—being in uniform does help—from an old farmer by the look of him, with an old dog in an old Buick. Everything about him was old. He was a nice bloke, said he lived near the border and that the main road to Spokane, USA, was not far from his place. He also said we'd find it much easier to get lifts if we split up into pairs, which seemed a good idea.

His farm was a really run-down sort of place, it looked like so many of the farms I'd seen on the movies. You know, when the young hero shows his bride her new home. The look on her face usually tells the story; broken machinery, fences, sheds and houses that always seemed to have a crooked look about them. She usually says, 'Lovely'—smiling through her tears.

'Yer better have a drink with me before yer go—help to keep the cold out while yer waitin' for a lift. I've got some home brew. Apple Jack.'

Bloody cider, I thought. What we all needed was a real drink like whisky, to keep us warm.

'Jest sip it gently,' he said, as he handed us glasses with some murky-looking liquid in them. He obviously didn't know he was talking to some pretty hardened drinkers. 'Good luck.'

'Cheers,' from all of us and we took a mouthful.

'Shit, bloody hell,' I gasped. 'What's this stuff made of?' I croaked, as coughs and choking noises came from the others.

'Apples. We fill a barrel with apple juice and throw it out into the snow in mid-winter. It freezes, except for a small amount in the middle about the size of a football. We then drill a hole through to the centre, syphon out the liquid there, which is pretty near pure alcohol. Apple Jack. Like I said, sip it.'

Two hours later, we staggered to the highway, very warm and very pissed. Syd and me would go together. We'd all arranged to meet at the main YMCA in Los Angeles.

We wandered down the road about 300 yards away from Nig and Johnny.

I'm sure it was the uniforms with 'AUSTRALIA' flashes on our sleeves and the fact that American troops were being well looked after in Australia that helped us on our way.

Also, in the States along the highways were signs saying 'GIVE A SERVICEMAN A LIFT'. We were travelling faster than the train and each driver seemed to be straight out of an American movie. The hospitality was great, we weren't allowed to pay for a thing.

It was just before we got into Spokane that Siddy said, 'Snow, yer know that dunny, beside the road that I went to about fifty miles back?'

'Yeah.'

'Well, that's where I think I left the money belt with all our dough.'

Syd had thought our money'd be safer with him, in a money belt.

'Shit, Syd, are yer sure?'

'Yeah, I remember hangin' it on a nail, when I dropped me strides.'

The driver, Lee Kilensky, pulled into the next gas station and made a phone call. It was to the radio station in Spokane. They said they'd put it over the air and there might be a chance somebody would find it and return it to the station.

Lee dropped us off at the radio station to wait for any news. He said he had to go on and

handed us a fifty dollar bill with his card wrapped inside.

'It's only a loan. If yer get through the war, yer can pay me back.'

'No worries. We'll pay yer back before they start shootin' at us. Thanks.'

I reckon we'd been waiting for a couple of hours, when one of the radio people came up to us and said the 'toilet', as he put it, had been checked out and 'no money belt'. Whoever found it kept it. 'Sorry about that. Will you be alright?'

'Yeah sure, we'll be alright.'

Aw strewth. Now what do we do—go on or go back? Our minds were made up for us.

'Can I help? I'm from the Salvation Army. My name is Irwin. I heard yer story on the radio and came to the station hoping you'd still be here.'

By now it was nearly midnight and he looked like he'd just got out of bed.

Well, the Salvos did us proud. They put us up in a motel for the night and made sure that we ate a typical American breakfast, which was huge.

Irwin joined us for coffee, wished us luck and handed Siddy a pamphlet all about the Salvation Army.

'Irwin. We don't know how to repay yer for all this. But thanks,' I said.

'Yer don't have to thank me. Just do me a favour and promise to read that pamphlet some time. Okay?'

'Okay. We promise. Thanks again.'

You can't beat them. They never missed a chance to push that old religion bit.

Irwin took us to the edge of town to the main highway heading towards San Francisco. Within five minutes we got a lift.

If only she wouldn't turn her head when she was talking to us because every time she did, the car went over the centre line onto the wrong side of the road.

She was about fifty, wearing a man's hat and raincoat and I reckon she was slightly crazy. She said she was going all the way to Oakland, California, to see her daughter—and by the look of it mostly on the wrong side of the road.

'Talkin' keeps me awake,' she said. 'My name's Beatrice, by the way.'

'This is Syd and I'm Vincent.'

If one of us could've sat in the front seat, it would've helped things a bit. She wouldn't have

146

had to turn her head so far around. But that seat was taken up by a huge dog, a mixture, by the look of him, of Alsatian and something very big. He just sat there staring straight ahead. Like a statue. Maybe it was her driving; perhaps he was just scared stiff.

'There's a bag of apples and some home-made ginger beer in the front. Help yourselves. I don't eat any of that crappy food from the gas stations while I'm drivin'.'

Syd and me looked at each other. Put our hand over the front seat and take some apples? She must be joking! We were hungry and thirsty I know, but the thought of being a one-armed air gunner . . .

'What about the dog? Will he bite?' I asked.

'His name is Rex,' she said very firmly. And so help me, he turned his head and looked at her. 'Rex, these nice young Australian airmen are gonna have some of our apples and ginger beer. Okay?'

I know I'm going crazy—but I swear Rex nodded his head.

'Okay. Reach over and take some apples and a demijohn of ginger beer.'

Syd and me hesitated a bit.

'Go on. He won't bite.'

Here goes I thought, and reached over to a corn bag full of apples. Rex didn't even bother to look. Encouraged, I quickly handed Syd about a dozen huge red apples and a large demijohn of ginger beer. Nothing seemed to be small in this car.

Beatrice kept munching apples and talking non-stop. She'd always leave about a third of the apple and give it to Rex, who in a sort of slow-motion action, gently took it, gave it one crunch and swallowed it. I'd never seen a dog eat apples before.

When you're only eating apples and drinking ginger beer in a car that's swerving all over the road, it kind of builds up a lot of gas inside you, which was giving me a gut-ache and there's only one way to get rid of it. But difficult in a car with a lady driver.

Beatrice might have seen our problem in the rear-view mirror, or maybe she had a problem of her own because she suddenly slammed on the brakes and yelled, 'Nature calls, here's a good spot.'

Rex went one way, Beatrice another and Syd and me in opposite directions—all running.

None of us, including Rex, had time to get out of earshot before four of the loudest farts followed by several smaller ones broke the silence of the clean American countryside.

And that's how it was from then on. 'The Oregon Trail'.

At one stage Siddy, I think to take his mind off the on-coming traffic and Beatrice's driving, suddenly found religion and pulled out the Salvation Army pamphlet that Irwin had given him and started reading it.

'Snow . . . Look!'

Syd had the pamphlet open and there, neatly folded between the pages, was a brand-new twenty dollar bill. He turned the next page . . . another twenty dollar bill.

'Nice people, eh.'

'Yeah, nice people,' I said feeling guilty and thinking back to the times when a bunch of us would throw stones onto the Salvos' tin roof during their prayer meetings in their small hall in Moree.

The drone of Beatrice's voice; the munching of apples; the cries of 'Nature calls!'; the gas stations; dozing in the back, too scared to go to sleep—and the miles rolled by. Pine forests,

sparkling rivers, logging camps, small towns straight out of the Wild West, real cowboy and Indian country—Klamath Falls, Mt Shasta, Red Bluff.

'Next big town is Sacramento. Not long now. We'll be in Oakland for breakfast.'

I've got to say Beatrice did us proud. She fussed around and mothered us. So different from that crazy driver we'd spent the last thirty hours with. Her daughter, whose husband was in the Marines, was just the same. Made us so welcome anybody would've thought we'd just won the war. A hot shower, ham and eggs for breakfast and we were ready to hit the road. It was good to feel clean again.

We politely refused Beatrice's offer of some apples to take with us. I think she understood.

He was as black as the ace of spades, had teeth as white as snow and apart from Primo Carnero was one of the biggest men I'd ever seen.

'Man, I gotta tell you, my son's havin' a great time in Australia. He's in the artillery and buckin' for sergeant. Where you boys headin'?'

'The YMCA in Los Angeles.'

'That's where yer goin' then,' he said.

He dropped us right at the door. 'Good luck, boys.'

A wave and he was gone. His furniture-removal truck seemed to take up the whole road ... Never did know his name.

There was a message on the noticeboard at the YMCA:

LAC BALL AND HILL, RAAF.

SO WHAT KEPT YOU? WE'RE IN ROOM 84.

NIG & JOHNNY

The buggers had beaten us down here.

For hospitality you can't beat the Yanks. I think every person we met tried to outdo all the others so that our stay in LA and Hollywood went by very quickly in a sort of haze of hang-overs. Every night we went to the Hollywood Canteen where we met and danced with film stars we'd only ever seen on the screen or in film magazines.

They were even more attractive off-screen than on. They had a sort of glamour about them and they weren't snooty at all but friendly and charming. Maybe I mistook this for something else because I asked Joan Leslie if I could take her home and was ever so nicely turned down.

'We aren't allowed to go out with service-men from the Canteen—no matter how nice they are. Sorry.'

What can you say to that?

I'd been in love with Deanna Durbin for years and I had three dances with her. It was like a dream. All it needed was for her to suddenly break into song. Bette Davis took my address in Australia and said she'd write to Mum tellin' her how well I looked.

How *well* I looked?

Syd reckoned my eyes were like 'pee holes in the snow' and no wonder. Each night, after the Hollywood Canteen closed, we'd go on to the Florentine Gardens, a nightclub, where it seemed Australian airmen were most welcome. All on the house. Even the hangover.

We met an Australian actress, Joan Winfield, who took us under her wing and organised trips to Paramount and Twentieth Century Fox studios. We watched Betty Hutton doing scenes with Eddie Bracken in *The Miracle of Morgan's Creek* and Loretta Young and Alan Ladd in *China*—or to be more honest, Alan Ladd's double doing most of the work, diving time after time into a tank of water made up to look like a creek.

Seemed pretty simple to me, even I could've done it. Maybe Alan Ladd couldn't dive.

It was strange walking around the studios seeing film stars like Claudette Colbert; standing with Walter Pidgeon and Joan Leslie selling War Bonds from a platform on Sunset Boulevard. All of us being treated like someone important and signing autographs. Watching the Crosby and Hope radio show and being given a pipe by Bing Crosby.

But as that corny old saying goes, 'All good things come to an end'. It was time to go back to Canada and get on with the bloody war. To quote Fitzpatrick at the end of his travelogues: 'And so we say a reluctant farewell to Hollywood ...'

I never did see a cowboy.

We took a bus through the famous Beverly Hills to Santa Monica, a lovely little town right on the ocean. When we stepped out of the bus, Syd and I had one dollar between us. It was Christmas Day.

Syd wanted to try the coast road on the way back.

Why not?

We didn't know that fewer cars travelled

the coast road and we were in trouble right from the start. Short rides and finally arriving in Santa Luis Olista broke and hungry.

Thank God there was a United Services Organisation there, where we got a feed and made friends with an army sergeant who insisted that we go back to camp with him. When we arrived we got a great reception. Mind you, there was a party going on and everybody was pissed.

An officer made a speech about how they thought the Australian soldiers were the greatest fighters in the world. We didn't argue.

Then Syd got up and said the same thing about the Yanks, which went down pretty well.

Boxing Day and another hangover. I dunno what it is about me but I get the feeling drinking doesn't agree with me. I always seem to be having a good time—until I wake up next morning. Maybe you have to be older?

It was getting colder now and Syd and me had to walk up and down by the side of the road to try to keep warm. Every time I stamped my feet the top of my head practically lifted off.

Luckily we hitched a ride right to San Francisco. We were getting a bit worried about arriving back to camp in time so we didn't stay

in 'Frisco but crossed the famous Golden Gate
Bridge and got a lift for about a hundred miles
to Ukail and slept that night in an empty bus
which was parked near a garage.

We had ten cents left after breakfast.

Not much traffic on the road. I guess they
were all at home in front of their warm fires,
recovering from their Christmas celebrations.

Finally we were given a lift to Eureka,
passing through some of the most beautiful
country: mountains and thick forests of the
Oregon Red Pines, which are the biggest trees in
the world. The road passed right through the
middle of one of them.

The United Services Organisation at Eureka
took care of our hunger, God bless them. Then
onto Crescent City where our driver insisted on
paying for our motel.

We took his address and promised to pay
him back. At the rate we were handing out IOUs,
we'd have to survive the war to repay them all.

After Crescent City, we decided to strike
inland to reach the main highway. It was
growing colder and colder and the rain hadn't
stopped for two days. We got a ride for about
twenty miles until we came across a landslide,

which would take about a day to clear.

By now we were really beginning to panic; we were running out of time so we climbed over the landslide and hitched a lift with a chap who was driving back to the main highway. Just before we reached the highway, he pulled up at a small cafe and said he was going to have something to eat and asked if we wanted anything. Not having any money we said no, we weren't hungry, we'd just have a cup of coffee. I think this was the worst part of the trip. We were actually starving and we had to watch him plough through a huge meal leaving a lot of it on his plate. He paid for our coffee. I had a terrible feeling that when he asked us if we were going to eat, he was asking us to have dinner on him.

We arrived at Grants Pass and then the main highway at about four o'clock. It was icy cold and we walked, trotted, jumped up and down for about two hours to stop ourselves from freezing and it was beginning to get dark. Soon we wouldn't have any chance of getting a lift.

It must have been the St Christopher medal I wore, because out of the murk a car pulled up

and the driver said he was going to Portland and did we want a ride?

Breakfast was in Eugene where we spent our last ten cents on a packet of salted peanuts.

Portland and it was still raining. We went to the YMCA to see if we could get a free bed. It was one o'clock in the morning. No worries—bed *and* breakfast. I really take my hat off to the Yanks.

I suppose the sight of a couple of Aussie airmen stamping up and down beside the road trying to keep warm would invoke a certain amount of sympathy. Well, that's what we were hoping and it worked for our next lift.

A 'sporting man', he said he was. His car was big, he was big and his business was big. He owned hundreds of slot machines all over the country and spent most of his time driving round collecting his money. He picked us up in the rain and we finally ended up in a snowdrift at a place called Cascade Locks. Snowbound—that's all we needed. We'd have to wait for a snowplough to come through to clear the road.

While we waited, our sporting friend was noisily getting drunk in a bar, joined by a couple of ladies who seemed intent on relieving him of

as much money as they could. Syd and me were starving. It was a real dump of a place, a few sailors and soldiers, some girls and half-a-dozen slot machines.

'Keep the winnings,' our new friend said, handing Syd a container of quarters, about $3. Our bloody pride wouldn't let us buy food and so we used the money as he intended.

His machines had it all back in about ten minutes.

'The two sailors over there wondered if you'd like to join them for some food—on the Navy.'

The waitress was young and pretty and for just a couple of seconds I forgot I was hungry.

'Yes. We'd love to,' said Syd, bringing me back to reality.

Put four fellows in service uniforms and right away they have something in common. We got on like a house on fire. They were nice guys, friendly, generous and they knew we were hungry. Two new friends and we all promised to keep in touch.

'There's a bus following the snowplough,' said our sporting friend. 'I'm gonna give you your fare to Calgary. A Greyhound bus to

Spokane and then the train to Calgary. And I don't want any arguments.'

We didn't argue.

'Give us yer address so we can pay yer back,' said Syd.

Our friend, who was well pissed by now, did his nut. 'You young guys are fighting for my wife and kids, it's the least I can do. But if yer could at some time drop a line to me and my wife, I'd more than be repaid.'

We promised. Drunk or sober, he was a decent sort of bloke.

Four-hundred miles to Spokane by Greyhound bus, 23 hours by train to Calgary, arriving 31 December at 2300 hours—New Year's Eve, 40 degrees below zero, broke, hungry and three days late. Here we go again.

At the bus depot we managed to borrow our fare to the camp from a couple of airmen. The Service Police at the guardhouse were expecting us.

'You're AWL and our orders are that you spend the night in gaol until you go before the CO at 1500 hours tomorrow. Happy New Year.'

'Corp, we're bloody starvin'. Any chance of

somethin' to eat? Anythin'?' I pleaded.

He just turned his back and walked away. Twenty minutes later he presented us with two of the biggest sandwiches I think I'd ever seen.

'Corp, yer blood's worth bottlin'. Happy New Year.'

We froze. We slept on the floorboards, no pillow and three very thin blankets.

The Corporal of the Guard marched us into the CO's office.

'Attention. LAC Ball, LAC Hill. Sir.'

'Well,' said the CO. 'Tell me about it.'

He sounded quite friendly but I'd heard it all before. I remember seeing people behaving like that in the movies, just before they gave the orders to shoot you.

We told him all about the trip down and the trip back. The people we'd met, we didn't leave out a thing. What with losing our money, landslides, snowbound, starving, freezing, we really painted a hard-luck story. We didn't lie, we simply told the truth and waited for the axe to fall.

The CO looked at us for a bit. Then he said, 'That's it?'

'Yes, sir,' we said together.

He dismissed the charge without loss of pay or a black mark on our conduct sheet. Nig and Johnny, who had arrived two days late, had been fined three days' pay and were confined to barracks for ten days. There's a lesson I should have learnt somewhere there—'*Always tell the truth*'.

It had been a great trip ... and I'd seen Hollywood.

SIX

OFF TO FIGHT
THE HUN

THE GUNNERY SCHOOL at Lethbridge, flying
in long-nosed Blenheims, and the cramped gun
turrets that always smelled of vomit. Most of us
at one time or other had been airsick. You were
supposed to clean up the turret after you but you
were always feeling so lousy that you never did
a good job.

The heavy smell of oil, fuel and gunpowder
and the odd piece of tomato or whatever in the
gunsight didn't help. Trying to hit the drogue, the
target towed by another aircraft, and being sick
at the same time wasn't easy. Yet somehow or
other we all passed; it seems all you had to do was
fire in the general direction of the target. There
was a rumour that because gunners were in short
supply, they never failed anybody anyway.

We had a passing-out parade, were given
our half-wing, three stripes, had a piss-up and

headed for Lachine near Montreal, then on to New York for a week's leave.

There were eight of us sleeping in one double room at the Piccadilly Hotel; visiting the Stage Door Canteen every night and only accepting invitations that said, 'Supper will be served'. We watched a skinny young bloke at the Paramount Theatre singing a few songs before the main picture came on but the squeals and yells of the bobby-soxers in the first five rows made it very hard for us to hear the words. He seemed pretty good nevertheless. His name was Frank Sinatra.

Back to Lachine to be given our postings to the business end of the war. Mine was to Coastal Command and I'd be doing my operational training at Nassau in the Bahamas. What a rough old war.

We waited two weeks in Miami before being shipped over to Nassau. Miami at that time had been taken over by the American Army; whose soldiers seemed to spend all day marching around the streets singing. They looked very fit and very serious. Maybe they'd been told they were off to fight in the jungles of the Pacific.

Apart from forming up into crews, training on Mitchells and finally moving on to Liberators, our time at Nassau was like being on a very exotic holiday camp: swimming in the clear blue waters of the Caribbean; being served tea by the Duchess of Windsor; a pep-talk by the Duke on arrival; the whispered invitations by beautiful girls as we walked back to camp at night.

I dunno about this war, or maybe I was just growing up and quite normal, but getting in and out of bombers and learning this and that about the many ways of killing people all seemed pretty easy. Most of us, or 99.9 per cent of us, spent more time thinking about girls than we did about the war. I reckon it's the uniform that does it. When we should have been thinking about King and country we had, instead, an obsession for blondes, brunettes and redheads.

Back to Miami for a week, then on to Moncton, New Brunswick, in Canada for a few days and finally New York, the *Queen Mary* and 20,000 American troops. At last we were off to England and the war. I wondered how many of us would survive.

Because of its speed the *Queen Mary* didn't need an escort. There was a rumour that we were being chased by U-boats, so instead of sailing straight across the Atlantic we went in a sort of arc.

Finally we steamed up the Clyde in Scotland, disembarked and packed onto a train for Brighton on the south coast of England, the receiving centre for all Aussie airmen. The RAAF had taken over the Imperial and Grand hotels there.

On the first night, I was in the bath on the top floor of the Grand Hotel when the air-raid sirens went off. You were supposed to go to the shelter in the basement seven floors below. I'm no hero but the thought of running half-naked to the shelter was too much—I just soaked in the bath till the all-clear.

Rationing, English beer, English girls, London and then Thorney Island, Hampshire, for more operational training. Finally I was posted to RAF Squadron No. 547. It was a mixed squadron made up of Commonwealth airmen, like our crew of one Scot, six Poms and three Aussies.

Siddy was posted to 53 Squadron, and both 53 and 547 Liberator squadrons would operate out of St Eval, Cornwall.

Dear old Syd went 'missing' on 4 February 1944, his third operation.

When a mate got the chop we did the usual thing, maybe in the mess or the village pub: toasted 'absent friends', remembered all the good things and forgave all the bad things about them until we were maudlin drunk and eventually staggered off to bed feeling that we had given our mate a 'send-off' in the only way we knew how. Deep down the feeling of guilt, that 'Thank God it wasn't me', was always there.

We sat in the corner of the public bar acknowledging the many condolences: 'Poor old Syd'—'Sorry about Syd'—'Tough about Siddy', as though we were the official receivers of sympathy. Somehow we didn't want intruders. We were his close mates and it was as if we had some special right to feel sorry for our friend without any distractions. We just wanted to wallow in our misery on our own.

We toasted Siddy and said, 'Do you remember ...?' at least a hundred times and washed those memories down with whisky and beer chasers until our friendly landlord eased us out the door.

'Gentlemen, I have to close. I'm sorry.'

We didn't talk much on the way back from the Ship Inn. It was bloody cold and each of us was wrapped in his own alcoholic thoughts.

Yer silly bugger, Siddy, why did you have to go and get yourself killed? You were one of the good guys. You'd only been married a couple of weeks before you joined up and all through Canada, the Bahamas, New York, Hollywood and England you'd never taken a girl home or even taken one out for that matter, while the rest of us were tearing around like chooks with their heads cut off trying to discover what girls were all about. Not that we ever found out.

You were always with us, joining in the drinking and dancing and then quietly slipping away back to camp, sometimes tapping my arm and saying, 'Snow, all your taste is in your mouth.' I dunno Siddy. I always thought my girls looked pretty good. Being married gave you a certain something. I dunno what it was. Maybe maturity, calmness, you never seemed to get angry. It was as if you had some special inner secret, a sort of contentment.

The love of your wife and your love for her, I suppose. Maybe I'd be like you one day. I'd like to think so—but then again, you old bugger,

you were special. So perhaps that's wishful thinking on my part.

Shit, it was cold! Bloody freezing! Already the frost was turning the fields white. Suddenly Ken Caldwell, the 'Professor', threw up his arms and yelled at the night sky, 'Fuck the war!'

Johnny, Nig, Bottle and I joined in and the Cornish countryside on that dark and frosty night echoed with the cry from five drunken airmen:

'Fuck the war ... Fuck the war ... FUCK THE WAR ...'

Gradually we lapsed back into silence, retreating once more into our own thoughts and trudged on, with about another half mile to go.

Siddy, it was only last night that I sat on your bed and talked to you as you were getting ready to go on operations. I can't remember what we talked about, nothing really, just two mates having a yarn. But I do remember you slipped a small photo of your wife into your battledress pocket, saying it was your lucky charm.

I tell you, I was bloody surprised, mate, because when I go on bloody ops I have so many holy cards, holy medals and scapulas on me, I sort of clank. Every letter I get from home has a

holy medal in it. A bloody bullet wouldn't get through that lot, I can tell you. It wouldn't dare try.

And when I asked if that was all you took, you said it was all you needed.

Yeah, well, it looks like you needed a bit of luck too. And then you said, 'Have fun at the dance. I'll see yer tomorrow.' And I said, 'Yeah. See yer tomorrow. Bye.' You said 'Bye' and that was it. Doesn't seem much to hang onto, does it?

Yeah, remember that trip we did to Hollywood and back and remember the time we were ... yeah, remember ...

I'll write to your wife. I think she oughta know about the photo and I'll tell a few lies and say what a nice bloke you were, but she'd know that. Silly bugger, Siddy, getting killed. Hope it was quick, mate.

I was living off camp at the Treyarnon Bay Hotel, teaching the Wrens who were stationed nearby how to surf ... sandy beaches, moonlight walks, village pubs ... Apart from the ops, lectures on first aid, VD, bombing and gunnery practise, it was like another holiday camp.

The number of frightening films we'd seen warning us about the perils of the dreaded VD and usually illustrated by a 'John Thomas' in the final disgusting stages of syphilis were too numerous to mention. The way they carried on, it seemed we didn't have a chance of surviving the war anyway. If the 'Jerry' didn't get us, the dreaded 'Pox' would. And those bombing practise sesssions—we'd lost Mitchell and Liberator crews in the Bahamas and here we were, still at it, diving on buoys along the Welsh coast, dropping 10 pound practise bombs and blazing away with our .5s trying to get it right. One could get killed. Which brings me to 'Shagger' Owens, the other Australian wireless air gunner in our crew. The name 'Shagger' is self-explanatory; his reputation as a 'ladies' man' was spoken of in awed tones by the rest of 547 Squadron.

He was *big* in every sense of the word. And those of us who'd been privileged to shower with him never really recovered. We'd come out of the showers in a state of shock and had an inferiority complex for the rest of our lives. So when, on a bombing practise trip, there was an explosion down aft and Shag screamed over the intercom, 'Fire, I'm hit', I was propelled in sheer panic to

the rear of the aircraft, which was full of smoke and fire-extinguisher liquid. We sprayed everything and everybody until eventually it cleared enough for us to see Shag lying unconscious between the beam guns. White-faced, eyes open, tongue hanging out the side of his mouth and the lower half of his body covered in blood—he was obviously dead. The blood seemed to be coming from his private parts. I believe at that moment we all thought, Oh no, not his pride and joy, never mind about the rest of him dying. We cut, tore, ripped his trousers off and there it was in all its glory, intact. We wasted seconds staring in relief, before realising that blood was still gushing from a wound near his groin. We placed a gauze pad over it, wishing we'd kept awake in all those first aid lectures, and three of us kept the pressure on the wound while at the same time trying to find out if his pulse was beating, which is very difficult in a vibrating, noisy, smoking aircraft screaming back to base.

The fire brigade covered the flaming aircraft in foam, cut it in two and the doctors pumped three and half bottles of plasma into Shag on the way to the hospital. He survived, but lost a couple of toes from gangrene.

During these bombing practise trips the rear of the aircraft was usually covered with 10 pound bombs just lying around on the floor. We even used to walk on them; apparently they were supposed to be safe. Shag stepped on a faulty one, which exploded and a piece of shrapnel pierced his main vein and artery near his groin, missing his 'pride and joy' by a hair. As he said, 'What's a couple of toes anyway.'

Then along came D-Day.

Fly eight, sleep eight, fly eight, sleep eight. Backwards and forwards across the Channel, protecting the flanks of the invasion forces. Thanking God that I wasn't down there in the mayhem of the Normandy beaches.

We had stripped our aircraft of everything in order to carry more ammunition, bombs and depth charges, and had been confined to camp for three days, so we had a pretty good idea what was coming. The whole of the south coast was jammed with landing craft.

After D-Day there was no longer any need for secrecy, so it was back to Treyarnon Bay and the Ship Inn at St Merryn, our favourite watering hole.

I left the pub in the company of a young

lady and, much the worse for wear from the dreaded booze, we sat down in the middle of a cornfield to have a 'bit of a yarn'. Suddenly we were bathed in light and a very angry lady was waving a torch about and yelling at the girl, calling her terrible names, 'You slut, Betty! And your fiance fighting on the beaches of Normandy!'

I think that was my most frightening and vulnerable moment of the war. Caught in a searchlight in that field of stubble and trying to run with my pants round my ankles.

Next day, on ops, looking down at the lines of supply ships and landing craft going back and forwards to Normandy, I thought, wherever you are, Betty's fiance, nothing happened last night. I just had 'bad intentions'. Good luck!

As gunners we were allowed, if we wanted, to carry a service revolver with us on ops, a 45, just like the Yanks. In theory, I suppose, the powers that be thought that if we were shot down over enemy territory we could then fight our way out of trouble. With a 45? Maybe Buck Jones, Tim McCoy and Tom Mix could but not yours truly, who had quite recently discovered that he wasn't

particularly heroic—a hand straying accidently near your gun and bang, you're dead! We'd heard stories of airmen being shot down and because they were wearing a gun Jerry didn't take any chances, they just shot them, no questions asked.

I didn't carry a gun.

Some did of course, and one gun-happy idiot, much the worse from the dreaded drink, started playing Russian roulette with his trusty 45 in his sleeping quarters and ended up shooting another gunner, who was lying on his bunk reading a book, in the leg. How unlucky can you get?

'What did you do in the war, Daddy?'

'Oh, I got shot in the leg by one of our chaps!'

Flight Lieutenant John Stewart, our skipper, was a keen, conscientious and, I thought, excellent pilot. Which, as a member of his crew, was very important to me. We had a pretty good understanding: he did his job and I did mine. The same applied to the rest of the crew. The more efficient we were, the better our chance of survival.

Well, as the saying goes, 'You could have knocked me over with a feather'.

'Ball, why don't you apply for a commission? I'll recommend you. The adjutant will tell you how to go about it.'

Hoping the stunned look didn't show too much, I replied as coolly as possible, 'Thanks, skipper. Yes ... er ... I'd like to have a go.'

Me an officer? Crikey ... but I dunno ... there are a lot of officers who are real drongos.

The adjutant gave me a form to fill in and said I'd have to have a letter from the education officer saying that I was a 'fit and proper person' to hold a commission.

This might be a bit of a worry because I left school when I was fourteen. But then again, the education officer played outside-centre and I played inside-centre and we were playing the Fleet Air Arm base at St Merryn the next day.

I don't think the education officer had received so much ball in a game of Rugby in all his life. I played like I've never played before: I was always looking for him, trying to put him into openings, backing him up, slipping him passes when I should have gone myself.

He scored two tries and was involved in two others. I've never seen a chap looking so pleased with himself. He was a bloody sight better than the *other* outside-centre at Bradfield Park who had 'helped' to shape my Air Force career.

When we were having a beer afterwards with the Fleet Air Arm lads, I managed to get him alone and while I was filling his glass from a jug of beer, I asked, 'Could I have a word with you, sir?'

'Of course, Snow.'

'Well, it's sort of official, sir.'

'Oh, er ... alright, Warrant Officer.'

'I'm applying for a commission and I need a letter from you either saying I am or am not a fit and proper person to hold a commission.'

He looked at me for a bit. 'Leave it with me ... er, Warrant Officer. I'll deal with it tomorrow.'

I hoped he was thinking, A good report means *lots* of ball in future games ... a bad report means little or *no* ball in future games.

A week later, I stood to attention in front of the first of the Commission Boards. There were two group captains and a squadron

leader. I knew them all, one was my commanding officer. They were reading and passing round a letter between them. God only knows what was in it, because they kept looking at the letter and then looking at me with raised eyebrows.

'We would like to ask you a few questions, Warrant Officer,' said my CO.

'Yes, sir?'

He stared at me for a bit and then asked, 'Er ... Now ... er ... What are they doing about the rabbit pest in Australia?'

I thought he was joking at first but looking at his face I realised he wasn't.

'Sir, they're shootin' 'em, poisonin' 'em, gassin' 'em, buildin' rabbit-proof fences to try and contain 'em, trappin' 'em and ... er ... '

'Thank you, Warrant Officer.'

Then, 'Are the rules of Rugby Union the same in England as in Australia?' This came from the squadron leader who often refereed our games.

'Yes, sir.'

'Thank you, Warrant Officer Ball. That will be all.'

I couldn't believe it. Some of the English

chaps had been asked difficult technical questions about radio and radar.

The war went on, the Allies pushing the Germans further and further back into their beloved Fatherland—or what was left of it after the continual raids by the RAF at night and the Yanks by day.

In September 1944, our squadron was transferred to Leuchars, near Dundee, in Scotland, to try to bottle-up the German shipping and the U-boat route along the coast of Norway and also to operate in the Baltic and have a go at the U-boat pens at Danzig.

'Would Warrant Officer Ball please report to the CO's office!'

Aw, shit! I'll bet it's to tell me that I've failed the Commission Board!

'How are you, Ball?'

'Fine, thank you, sir.'

'Pretty fit and well?'

'Yes, sir, pretty fit.'

'Good. One of our chaps on the squadron's boxing team has had to drop out and we're looking for somebody about thirteen stone who is pretty fit. You play Rugby and swim for the

station and I was wondering if you'd like to take his place, for the sake of the squadron, y'know.'

'Me, sir? I'm not *that* fit, sir.'

I knew how long a three-minute round is. A bloody lifetime if you're not up to it.

'Oh, what a pity. Well, never mind. Oh, by the way, you did very well at the Commission Board at St Eval. It just needs my recommendation for you to see the Air Commodore when he arrives here next week and you should get your commission.'

This was bloody blackmail!

'Still, if you feel you're not fit enough ...?'

The bugger had me—and he knew it.

'I'll have a go, sir.'

'Good show, Ball. You're not on ops next Tuesday. I'll arrange your interview with the Air Commodore for then.'

'Thank you, sir.'

I saluted and left.

Bloody hell. Three, three-minute rounds. I'd been training on beer and whisky for the last three years. When I told Nig, Johnny and the Professor, they insisted that I start training right away and go to the gym.

Two days to get fit. I took a couple of

swings at the big punching bag and felt exhausted.

'Bugger this! Let's go to the pub and drown our sorrows.'

Which we did.

'Snow, we've found who you're fightin'. It's that big bloke in the white tracksuit who runs round the perimeter every day.'

I'd seen him. He sort of ran on his toes, shadow-boxing at the same time.

I got the dentist to make me a mouth-guard—at least there was a chance that I might keep *some* of my teeth.

In the ring he looked so fit and big and clean. He glowed with health and had on all the proper boxing gear, which fitted. I had on sand-shoes, long khaki shorts, a red sash and an off-white singlet. At least, I thought, the red sash would tone in with the blood—mine.

He did all that squatting up-and-down bit and pulling at the ropes. The way he was carry-ing on we wouldn't have any bloody ring left. He was just trying to scare me, and doing a very good job of it.

The bell sounded for the first round. Oh, Bluey Baker, where are you?

I reckon the first round was a draw. The second round he *just* won.

By the third round I couldn't raise my hands above my waist. The only thing I was protecting was my private parts. It all seemed to be in slow motion; I remember watching my mouthguard lazily floating across the ring. I didn't feel the punch and I was still on my feet at the final bell. In a dazed sort of way I thought, with a bit of training I could beat this guy.

They gave me a spoon—for coming second.

I'm stuffed if he asks me technical questions about radio or radar. I could operate them pretty well but I didn't have much of a clue about what went on inside their casings, and the questions were bound to be hard after those ones they'd asked about rabbits and Rugby at the first Commission Board at St Eval.

'Warrant Officer Ball.'

I stepped into the interview room and threw the best, smartest salute to the Air Commodore that I'd ever given in the whole of my Air Force career.

'How do you like it over here, Ball?' asked

the Air Commodore. He made it sound like I was on holidays.

How do you answer a question like that, in wartime? What I should've said was, 'Oh, very nice, sir. I'm havin' a lovely time. I'm thinkin' of comin' back again next year. It's a great war, sir.'

Instead I said, 'Very nice, sir. Scotland's a lovely place.'

'Would you mind closing that window a bit for me, Ball?'

'Yes, sir.'

I closed the window a bit for him.

'I understand you play a lot of Rugby. Do you know Captain Malan? He's South African.'

'Yes, sir, he's in the squadron team, on the left wing.'

'Good player, isn't he?'

'Yes, sir, very good.'

'I understand you're in the Scottish Services squad to play the RAF at Murrayfield.'

'Yes, sir.'

'Well, that's all, Ball. Glad you like it over here. Look after yourself.'

'Yes, sir. Thank you, sir.'

On the way back to the mess, I thought of

the three questions that would probably get me a flat hat. Not one of them had anything to do with the war! In fact, nobody even mentioned the war! Strange.

The bunk above me was empty. The Professor, Ken Caldwell, should have been back hours ago. Maybe they were diverted to another 'drome. I looked out of the window, clear blue sky, a beautiful day.

Shit, not another one. We hung round the ops room for a while. Still no word. He was five hours overdue. The date, 27 October 1944.

We went to his locker and took out the odd little personal things that he said we were to have if he got the chop. It was the same arrangement we all had. Something to remember him by. Not that we needed it.

Dear old Professor. What a bloody waste—it's always the good guys. We called him Professor for obvious reasons, he was older, wiser and had a steadying influence on the rest of us and now? Bloody war—Siddy—Professor. Who'd be next?

I wrote to his parents.

Three weeks later my commission came

through. Nig's too and we were given fifty pounds each to go to London to buy our officer's uniforms.

We booked in at the Strand Palace Hotel, which was the adopted hotel for Aussie aircrew on leave in London. It was just down the Strand from Australia House and a gentle stroll to Codgers pub, the famous watering hole for Aussie airmen.

We bought a tin trunk and a flat hat at the supply store in Australia House, planning to get the rest the next day. Unfortunately we went to the dogs at White City that night.

I don't know what it was about the dogs that I backed, but they either fell over, got bumped, lost interest or were just plain no good. One of the dogs I backed even made a pass at another dog in the middle of the race! His mind was definitely not on the job.

We lost all our money and were on the train back to Scotland the next day. The adjutant was quite surprised that Australia House, the largest supply store for Aussie airmen in England, didn't have uniforms to fit us!

Eventually we did get uniforms, made to measure by a tailor in Edinburgh.

Seven

GUINNESS, PEACH MELBA AND STEAK

VINCE, I'VE ENCLOSED the addresses of your great aunts and uncles in County Cork. If you ever get the chance, do go and see them.

Bette Davis, the film star, wrote me a lovely letter from Hollywood. She said, she met you at the Hollywood Canteen and that you were looking well. Wasn't that nice of her.

Look after yourself. God bless you
Your Loving Mother xxx

Gee, fancy Bette Davis writing! Mum, bless her, thinks that I can hop on a boat and go over to Southern Ireland just like that, forgetting that that particular country is neutral. Mind you, half the eligible male population of Southern Ireland are fighting with the British anyway.

I didn't understand it. The Irish are supposed to hate the British yet when a war begins, they join the British forces and fight alongside them.

I wonder how many Kennedys are in County Cork? If they are good Catholics, thousands I suppose.

'Hey, Mac. We've got ten days' leave comin' up. How about we spend some of it in Dublin's fair city and then go and see my relatives, the Kennedys of County Cork?'

Mac was our Canadian second pilot. A nice guy.

'Sure. Why not? How do we go about it?'

'We'll talk to Paddy Lynch. He's the flight engineer in Basil Key's crew. He'll gen us up.'

'Well,' said Paddy. 'First of all, you'll need civilian clothes but don't worry about that because I'll be lendin' you some of mine. Now, you get over to Belfast by hitching a ride in a Dakota—they're flying in and out of Leuchars all the time and going over to Aldergrove in Northern Ireland. Then you catch a train from Belfast to Dublin. It's as simple as that. Oh, and don't try to smuggle tea and other foodstuffs

into Southern Ireland. The Customs get on the train at the border and some of them are real bastards. And stay at the Gresham Hotel—it's one of the best in Dublin.'

Smuggle tea and other foodstuffs into Southern Ireland. I have to be honest, it hadn't really crossed my mind.

Everything went as Paddy predicted. It was standing room only on the train from Belfast to Dublin, and everybody in our carriage was trying to smuggle tea across the border. They were stuffing it under the seats, putting it in brown paper bags and hiding it under their hats and caps, even pouring it loose into their pockets. I'd never seen such drama over tea. Where did they get it from anyway? It was rationed in Britain.

'Would you two fine young gentlemen do an old lady a kind service? I can tell by looking at you, you're not Irish and you're wearing macintoshes with such lovely big pockets in them. Would you mind looking after some tea for me until the Customs men have been through? They get on at the border.'

Sure and Begorrah, I thought, 'tis 'Mother Macree' herself.

It had to be. She had the sweetest face and the softest Irish brogue you ever did hear. And she was still talking, 'I know you're servicemen and when the Customs come through, all you have to do is show them your identity cards and they won't bother you. God bless you both.'

Then, like she'd been doing it all her life, she slipped a half-pound packet of tea into each of our pockets and moved away into the crowd before we could protest.

Mac looked at me. 'Didn't Paddy say something about not smuggling tea?'

Tea containers of all shapes and sizes moved ahead of the Customs men, being handed from person to person and then splitting up and curling in two arcs behind them as the men moved down the carriage. I'm not sure about all this. I could see what was happening and there was so much suspicious-looking movement going on I couldn't understand why the Customs men didn't see it. Maybe it was some sort of strange Irish game they were playing.

They confiscated a token amount of food-stuffs from our carriage and then moved on to the next.

A gentle tug on my arm and there she

was—'Mother Macree' with her sweet smile and her extra-large handbag agape. We returned the four packets of tea.

'Ah, sure, you're two lovely gentlemen. God bless you both. I'll pray for you.'

And she disappeared once more into the crowd.

'Mac, if we can get the Irish prayin' for us, we're in with a pretty good chance of gettin' through this war because I reckon they've got a fair bit of pull up there.'

The carriage by this time was in the process of sorting out who owned what. They all seemed to end up getting back what they started with except for one burly chap who kept repeating in a loud aggressive voice, 'I'm still missin' a pound of Liptons.'

He was answered with a lot of innocent stares.

'I'm still missin' me tea.'

And he was still repeating it very angrily as we arrived in Dublin. 'I want me bloody tea!'

So this is Dublin's fair city.

    FIGHT POVERTY
    FIGHT CONSUMPTION

HELP THE TB APPEAL

HELP THE POOR

They were some of the posters we saw on the way to our hotel. Even when we got out of the cab, we were approached by a couple of beggars who were very quickly moved on by the doorman.

The Buttery at the Gresham Hotel was *the* place to be for the 'happy hour' before dinner.

Mac and I and the other 'civilians' were outnumbered by about two to one by priests who were enjoying the pleasures of the flesh in the form of Irish whisky and Guinness.

'Maybe there's some sorta priestly convention on here or somethin',' I said.

'Yeah, maybe,' said Mac. 'Let's hope the convention's over otherwise they're all going to be pissed by the time they get to it tonight.'

But there wasn't any convention and eventually we all moved into the dining room where Mac and I had a large T-bone steak each, followed by Peach Melba.

Now, my conscience can handle the fact that there are beggars in the street and I'm eating steak and Peach Melba in the dining room of the Gresham Hotel because I've been in a bloody

war and haven't seen a bloody steak for years.
But how do all these priests handle it?

Doesn't it bother them, as they tuck into
their steaks, Peach Melbas and Irish coffees, that
there's all that poverty outside in the streets? Do
they, as they walk along O'Connell Street, contribute to all those appeals for help?

Maybe it's a passing-out celebration. Yeah!
That's it, a passing-out celebration. But then why
aren't they all sitting together?

Mac and I floated along on a river of
draught Guinness, vaguely remembering names
like O'Reilly's, Murphy's Bar, The Irish Arms,
The Shamrock, Royal Hibernian, and being
looked after by friendly Dubliners and taken to
parties, the Guinness Brewery, the horse races
and, of course, Mass. We watched a drunken
Irishman being thrown out of a dance hall
because he'd said 'Up the IRA!'. I wasn't sure
whether he meant 'Up the IRA' as 'Good on the
IRA', or the 'Up Yours' kind of 'Up'. The bloke
who threw him down the twenty concrete steps
seemed to know.

During the 'Holy Hour', which was the
hour between three and four o'clock when the
pubs closed, I walked along one side of

O'Connell Street and Mac walked along the other, counting priests. We came up with thirty-four and thirty-six—a total of seventy.

It would seem that going into the priesthood was a profession, yet I was always told that you had to have a strong calling and vocation. It was all getting up my nose a bit, having boxes shoved at us in every pub we were in—help this, help that—and then joining the Fathers in The Buttery at the Gresham.

There was something wrong somewhere and I was starting to ask a few questions about the Catholic faith.

We never got to County Cork.

We never got out of Dublin.

We were bloody lucky to get back to our squadron, and it took us about a week to dry out.

Ah, this drink, it's a terrible, terrible thing.

I was still recovering from leave in Ireland and trying to come to terms with my religion, when I had a letter from Mum telling me that Noni, my beautiful young sister, who was fourteen, had decided to become a nun and would be going to the Sisters of Mercy at Parramatta

as a boarder until she took her initial vows when she was older.

I knew Mum and Dad couldn't afford to pay boarding fees for her and after my experience in Dublin with the Holy Fathers my devious mind was working overtime. Was 'free' board at Parramatta a kind of bribe to help Noni with her vocation?

I didn't like the idea of my little sister being closeted in a convent for the rest of her life and immediately wrote to Mum asking them not to do anything final until I got back from the war.

'Get off yer bum, Snow. I want yer to serve Mass.'

I managed to painfully open one eye and get into focus the owner of that familiar voice. Our Catholic padre was a big Irish second-row forward, a sort of gentle giant, who could mix it with the best of them on the Rugby field both vocally and physically.

'I don't feel well Padre and I've forgotten how to serve Mass.'

'That's one thing you never really forget. It's like riding a bike. Now off yer bum and get dressed.'

'Yes Padre.'

I slowly dressed, thinking: first there was
Dublin with its poverty and the young priests
with their steaks, Peach Melbas and Irish coffee.
Then a letter from Mum about Noni wanting to
become a nun and now I'm about to serve Mass
for our big Irish padre. It was as though I was
giving my approval for all of it.

'*Ad deum qui laetificat juventutem meam.*'

I wonder if having a hangover while serving
Mass is some kind of sin? Perhaps not the hangover but the cause of it—like over-indulgence?

'*Confiteor deo omniptenti* ... '

I wonder did you, Padre, go to The Buttery
at the Gresham in Dublin and did you, Padre,
contribute alms to the beggars along O'Connell
Street?

'*Et salutare tuum da nobis.*'

I wonder if maybe I was using my Dublin
experience as an excuse to give the Catholic faith
away, because it seemed a lot easier to get
through the war with the drinking and the girls
and not having to front up to confession every
now and then and listen to the stunned silence
from the padre as I trotted out my wrongdoings
since my last confession.

The padre called us 'his squadron of sinners'.

Yeah, maybe I wanted it both ways, because I made pretty sure that on each ops trip I wore all the scapulars, holy cards and medals that the family had sent me to keep me safe. 'My lucky charms' I told the rest of the crew as I clanked out to the aircraft. I always hoped and sometimes prayed that when things got a little rough somebody up there would intervene. I was sort of hedging my bets.

'*Et cum spirito tuo.*'

And what about all that Limbo bit, Padre? I never could quite believe that. I know a good Catholic just has to have faith and believe. Well you have to don't you, what with the mysteries like the Holy Ghost, the Virgin Mary and the Resurrection. But Limbo was the one I thought was a bit unfair. I was taught that you go to Limbo if you die when you're a baby and are not baptised. So what about all the babies in say, the Belgian Congo, whose parents had never heard of the Catholic religion and were happily into worshipping their sun and rain gods and other images. Idolatry? Did they go to Limbo for eternity? It seems to

me that if you were 'enlightened' you had four chances: Limbo, Purgatory, Heaven or Hell. But if you were 'unenlightened' you didn't have to worry about any of that and ended up with your ancestors in some happy hunting ground. And another thing, if God is all powerful and merciful Padre, what about the suffering and slaughter that's going on now? Why does He let it all happen?

Well, with the wondering and the worrying and the hangover and being in the process of losing my faith, I lost my place a few times and was brought to heel by a loud cough and glare from the padre.

'*Deo gratias.*'

The hundreds of times I'd served Mass and never queried what it was I was saying in Latin. I knew a bit of course, but I was like a mindless parrot, just repeating what I'd been taught.

No doubt the nuns translated it all when they were teaching me, when I was seven years old. And I suppose, if I had an enquiring mind, I could've looked it up in *My Sunday Missal* but I never did. I was always in a hurry, there was never time.

'Benedicat nos omnipotens Deus, Pater, et Filius Spiritus Sanctus.'

'Amen.'

I would have thought that by now, being in action, I'd be more concerned about survival than about girls. But no. Going on ops seemed to be just something that was fitted in between dates.

Maybe, at twenty, I was just growing up and quite normal. Or maybe it was the number of times I was made to sit with the girls at school as a form of punishment, when the misdemeanour I had committed didn't warrant the cane. The good sisters thought that the humiliation of 'sitting with the girls' would be a suitable punishment. Looking back on it now, I remember I rather liked it. Maybe that was what started me off?

Apart from playing the odd game of golf on the Old Course at St Andrews, Dundee was where we had our 'serious' recreation. The last train from there back to camp was about eleven-thirty pm. If you missed it, you had a choice: get a room for the night, if you were lucky, or catch the two o'clock milk train which didn't stop for

you, but slowed down on the small gradient going into Leuchars station. You had to jump out into the night hoping that you'd miss the steel stanchions that ran alongside the track. You're inclined to take chances when you've had a few, and after doing this a couple of times, and realising that we had a better chance of being killed beside the railway lines at Leuchars than we ever did flying, four of us booked a permanent room at the Railway Hotel, Dundee. Most of our 'entertaining' was done there and I suppose out of appreciation for all the money we spent, the hotel turned on a birthday party for me on 4 December 1944, my twenty-first. It was quite a night. Somehow nine of us managed to sleep in 'our' one room.

Jonesy and I had kept in touch. He'd just about finished his tour of ops as a mid-upper gunner in Lancasters and said it was a lousy job. 'I seem to spend most of my time over Berlin.'

By wheeling and dealing we managed to get a week's leave together and decided Edinburgh would be a good place to spend it.

We were in the pub early, having a hair of the dog, not saying much. Just staring into our

beer hoping the pain would go away.

'Wonder what happened to Bruce?'

'I dunno,' I said. 'The last time I saw him was in Brighton just after I arrived.'

'You never mentioned that before, Snow.'

'No, it's somethin' that I'm not very proud of. I was walkin' up the main street and I heard this familiar voice callin' out "Snow, Snow!" And there he was, Pilot Officer Bruce Burton, wings and all. You know, I couldn't spare him a few hours—not knowin' whether we'd ever see each other again—because I had a lousy date. And when you think that the three of us had played Rugby for Eastwood together, knocked around together, joined up together. Some mate I turned out to be. Wish I could turn the clock back now.'

'Yeah, I have to agree. You are a shit, Snow.'

'Yeah.'

Jonesy and I were at one end of the bar and a lone British Tommy was at the other.

'Let's ask him to have a drink with us.'

We moved along towards him.

'Would you join us for a drink?' I asked.

'Yes, sir. Thank you, sir. It'd be an honour.'

'Look, let's cut out the "sir" and "honour" bit, shall we? My name's Vince and this is Jonesy. What's yours?'

'John,' he said. 'No, I mean it. It's an honour to drink with any aircrew. I take me hat off to you blokes. You wouldn't get me up in one of those planes, too bloody dangerous. The ground's good enough for me.'

Jonesy had ordered three pints and as he pushed one towards John, he asked, 'Are you on leave?'

'Yeah. Sick leave. Bloody Jerry nicked me leg in Normandy with a bayonet.'

'When did you go over?' I asked.

'D-Day,' he said, swallowing half a pint of beer.

I looked at the Africa Star ribbon he was wearing and thought, I wouldn't be a bloody foot soldier for all the tea in China. Our new friend had, no doubt, been called up or volunteered, been given a gun, bayonet, helmet and some training. Then they would have put him in a landing craft, got him to run up a mined beach in North Africa and then fight his way across the deserts of the Middle East until Rommel's Afrika Corps was defeated. Then they would

have brought him back to England, put him in another landing craft and got him to run up the mined beaches of Normandy, being shelled and pinned down by enemy fire. He then would have advanced inland, fighting his way through the French villages until he came face-to-face with a big bloody German. They then would have proceeded to try to do each other in by sticking bayonets in each other. And he thinks flying is dangerous!

Jonesy and me were fighting an impersonal war. We never meet the enemy; no hand-to-hand fighting for us.

By the time our friend John said goodbye, we were happily drunk, swearing eternal friendship and, of course, promising to write.

Jonesy and I went our separate ways at the end of six days. He staggered off to catch his train back to Waddington and I, in the same condition, went back to Leuchars. If the war didn't get us, I reckoned the booze would.

Jonesy was a great mate and whenever possible I'd go down to Waddington to see him. There was this song 'Coming in on a Wing and a Prayer' and if it ever fitted anybody it was Jonesy.

About four weeks after the Edinburgh leave I managed to get down to see him and was greeted by a very changed man. His lips were swollen and covered in scabs, he had a black eye and limped. The scabs were the result of a little trip over Berlin.

He said, 'I was sittin' in my turret lookin' at the stars on my way to Berlin and I was feeling very drowsy. Well, that was understandable, I'd been givin' the old booze a bit of a bashin' lately and thought my lifestyle was just catchin' up with me. I suddenly realised there was somethin' wrong with my oxygen supply and I was on the verge of passin' out. Not thinkin' too clearly, I tore off my mask and jammed the small emergency oxygen bottle into my mouth. And you know what happens when metal touches flesh at 25,000 feet? It sticks. Not very bright, eh? And that's how I went to Berlin and back. They cut the oxygen bottle off my lips at the hospital.

'The black eye and limp? Ridin' my bicycle into a ditch on the way back from the pub. I'm thinkin' of givin' up the drink. You know, the day after I got back from our Edinburgh leave I spent a lot of time in the pub. I was on ops that night. Anyway, I got into the aircraft, settled into

my turret and we took off. I was thinkin' Berlin here we come, four more trips and my tour of ops will be over, bloody marvellous. Then somebody tapped me on the leg and said, "Come on Jonesy, get cracking—debriefing." What about . . . I then realised we were on the ground. I'd been to Berlin and back—asleep. You see why I'm thinkin' of givin' up the booze.'

He never did, of course.

'Skipper, four blips sixty miles, five degrees port.'

'What do you think they are?'

I mentally flipped a coin. At sixty miles they could be anything. 'Chances are they're U-boats, Skipper. They're not that far from the U-boat pens at Danzig.'

'Only one way to find out. Take a look,' he said.

We operated singly at night with a Leigh light; a type of searchlight under the starboard wing. The idea was that you'd home onto enemy shipping or U-boats by means of radar, losing height all the time and the Leigh light would be switched on about a quarter of a mile from the target. In theory it was supposed to blind,

surprise and frighten the hell out of them. If you can, imagine a bloody big four-engined bomber a few hundred feet above you, dropping bombs, depth charges and other nasties and you're lit up like a Christmas tree.

Of course, if you didn't home exactly over the target you were a sitting duck and usually a dead one.

I kept giving the distance and the bearing. 'Ten miles dead ahead. There are now five blips.'

Another wild guess: 'I think the two in the middle are U-boats and the other three escort vessels. I think one of 'em's a destroyer.'

'Skipper to crew. We're going in to attack.'

Oh shit, I thought, for God's sake and for all our sakes get it right this time, Ball.

'Five miles—1 degree port—steady, steady.'

'Four miles—dead ahead—steady.'

'Three miles—dead ahead—steady.'

'Two and a half miles—dead ahead—steady.'

'Two miles—steady.'

'One and a half—slightly to starboard.'

'One mile—dead ahead.'

'Three quarters—dead ahead.'

'Half—dead ahead.'

'Quarter—dead ahead.'

'Leigh light on. I can see them. Two U-boats, two escorts and a destroyer,' yelled the skipper.

By this time we were 200 feet above the water.

Then all hell broke loose. I could feel the aircraft shudder as we dropped our load over the U-boats and were hit by the gunfire from the U-boats, the destroyer and their escorts below.

All our guns were firing, eight .5s blazing away as we got to hell out of there.

'Number 3 engine's gone. I'm feathering it. Has anybody been hit?'

'Rear gunner. Okay, Skipper.'

'Beam gunners. Okay, Skipper.'

'Mid-upper. Okay, Skipper.'

'Nose gunner. Okay, Skipper.'

'Navigators. Okay, Skipper.'

'Radar. Okay, Skipper.' Just, I thought, feeling a hell of a draught above my head.

'Skipper, beam gunner here. I'm not sure, it's still too dark, but I think our starboard undercarriage is hangin' down.'

Shit, that's all we need. An aircraft full of holes, flying on three engines and probably no

undercarriage. Looks like Sweden, here we come. Great.

Sweden was a 'friendly' neutral country, which furnished us with our weather reports when we were operating in the Baltic. On our way to the U-boat pens at Danzig, we'd fly through the Skaggerak and over the southern tip of Sweden at about a thousand feet. To make it look good for the Germans, the 'friendly' Swedes would open fire with their ack-ack in front, behind, either side, but never at us.

Sweden always looked like a fairyland to us with all its lights. It was something we hadn't seen for years—people skating on the icerinks, cars whizzing along the highways—a country at peace.

On all these ops, we'd be issued with Swedish currency and most of us carried a clean shirt in our parachute bag. If you got into trouble and didn't think you could make it home, the idea was to bail out or land in Sweden, blow up your secret equipment and wait to be taken to an internment camp where, from all reports, you'd have a ball and then after about six weeks you'd be flown back to England by BOAC, a civil airline which was

still operating between England and Sweden.

'Skipper to crew. We do have a damaged undercarriage but wherever we go, Sweden or England, we're going to have the same problems. We should be able to manually crank down the port undercarriage and I'd rather land at a 'drome that I know. We can get home on three engines, we'll be there for breakfast.'

What he didn't say was, 'Besides, my wife is expecting a baby'.

So, for hours, we sat around an open bomb bay looking at the North Sea, ready to bail out or ditch. We'd been told that you lasted about twenty minutes in the North Sea in wintertime . . . and it was wintertime. Not something to think about.

But like they do in the movies, the skipper got us home. He made a great landing and we just walked away from the plane, giving the old Lib a thankyou pat as we left. Flight Lieutenant John Stewart, our skipper, got an immediate award of the DFC, the Distinguished Flying Cross.

I finally finished my tour of ops, fifty-three trips, and was posted to Aldergrove, Northern Ireland, as a radar instructor, at the ripe old age

of twenty-one. I was more scared as an instructor flying with these new crews then I ever was on ops. They all looked so young.

We were told three days before the official announcement. So by the time VE Day did arrive, the world had taken on a somewhat blurry look. Draught Guinness can do that.

The Australian Government, bless them, grounded all Australian aircrew. No more flying.

I'd made it.

eight

I Still Want to be a
Cowboy on the Films

'Sir, I would like a week's engagement leave.'

'Flying Officer Ball,' the officer said, looking at a long list in front of him, 'You are on the next draft home.'

'Yes I know, sir, but my girlfriend has just accepted me sir, last night on the phone, and I'd like to see her and her parents before I go, sir. You understand, sir? They live in Scotland, sir.'

'Alright Ball, I'll take you off the next draft.' The Transport Officer shook his head. 'I don't know, but nobody seems to want to go home.'

'Yes sir ... er ... no sir. Thank you, sir.'

He was dead bloody right. We were having such a good time in Brighton and the only way you could get off a draft home was to get

'engaged'. I don't remember seeing any airmen rushing around breaking their neck to leave England or saying things like, 'I can't wait to get at those bloody Japs.' Stuff that.

Finally they put their foot down, stopped all 'engagement leave', got us all together and packed us off to Liverpool and the *Mauretania*. We were homeward bound.

A lot of the chaps I trained with in Canada were on board so it was like old home week. We toasted absent friends, Siddy, Professor and others. There were moments of sadness.

As England receded into the distance, jumbled thoughts, pictures and regrets filled my mind. Engine noises, guns, pubs, lost mates, tracers lazily heading towards you, the patch-work quilt of the English countryside and the girls, ah the girls. Especially the WAAFs who were so much a part of our lives from that first day we joined 547 Squadron. I remembered my first real encounter with an English WAAF. She looked about fourteen. Her face was smooth and rosy and her voice low and inviting as she said, 'Do you want a leek? Do you want stuffing?'

I stammered a no to the first question and a yes to the second. She couldn't quite hide the

twinkle in her eyes as she gave me a dollop of seasoning.

It was lunchtime in the Sergeants' Mess at Thorney Island, Hants, Easter 1943.

I really don't believe the RAF could have operated as efficiently as it did without the WAAFs. I know we aircrew couldn't have. The WAAFs were our friends, our drinking mates, our mothers, our favourite aunts and sometimes lovers and future wives. They fed us, clothed us, packed our parachutes, consoled us, cheered us up and ticked us off. They drove us out to our aircraft and they'd be there waiting for us when we got back. I think we were all a bit in love with our transport drivers. There was always a cheerful, 'Good luck. Safe trip. I'll be waiting for you.' And they were.

I can't sing their praises enough. They did more for our morale than all the patriotic songs and speeches that ever came out of World War Two. My gratitude and thanks to all those lovely ladies. God bless.

I liked England and the people. I'd come back one day. I never did see a bloody German.

Maybe that was just as well. The thought of facing one, man to man, in mortal combat,

had always made my gut turn over. I don't think I'm the stuff heroes are made of.

I don't believe I joined up because of any great feeling of patriotism, 'to fight for my country, to stop the yellow horde' that I used to read about in *Chums Annual*, or to kill some Nazis and avenge the death of friends like Fred Fernside from across the road who had died with the AIF in the Middle East.

I really think I joined up because I wanted to be a fighter pilot and wear a nice blue uniform and get the girls. Also, a lot of my mates, like Jonesy and Bruce, were joining up at the time and it seemed the right thing to do. Maybe I joined for all the wrong reasons, but I did fight. I can't remember any of the blokes who I trained and flew with ever saying, 'I just can't wait to get at those bloody Germans,' or 'I can't wait to get at those bloody Japs.' I think we were all too shit scared.

When you multiply your lost mates with those of every other soldier, sailor and airman, including the enemy, then add all the dead civilians, plus the injured—God! So we beat Germany and we're already talking about fighting Russia and communism, and we haven't beaten the Japs yet.

Still, it was the war to end all wars. I'm glad I was part of it.

After the *Queen Mary*'s four-tiered bunks, hundreds to a deck, two meals a day and long queues for the dunny, the *Mauretania* was like a luxury cruise. We were four to a cabin.

Although jammed to the gunwales with airmen, ex-POWs from New Zealand and Australia, English brides and civilian personnel, we still got some of the best food I'd ever had, even a choice of dishes. Being an officer helped. Thank God I knew what they were doing about the rabbit pest in Australia!

There were lazy days of playing 500 and euchre, watching the soldiers at their favourite game—two-up—their boxing matches and the luxury of being a spectator, and trying to figure out which four girls had gone into the oldest profession in the world. They'd made the mistake of depositing large sums of money at the Purser's office about ten days out of Liverpool. Business apparently was very brisk, what with all those ex-POWs. The price list, so we were told, was five pounds a 'short time' and twenty-five pounds 'the night' and that was on life-jackets!

The captain was informed and business dropped off after the 'ladies' were restricted to certain areas and had a curfew put on them.

We arrived at Panama only to be told that there would be no shore leave as the Aussie troops on the ship before us had practically wrecked the town after an ex-POW soldier had been relieved of his money in some clipjoint. The soldier rounded up his mates and they then took out four years of the frustration of being POWs on this unfortunate town. Apparently they did quite a job on it.

The fascination of actually going through the canal, however, partly made up for the disappointment of no shore leave. Then it was on to Honolulu where an Aussie soldier was killed while 'directing' the traffic. After four years without a drink, the POWs found the booze hard to handle. To survive North Africa, a POW camp in Germany and then be killed by a car on the way home—how unlucky can you get.

As the *Mauretania* steamed slowly out of Honolulu, it was chased by about twenty small craft containing soldiers waving their slouch hats and cheered on by all of us on board. Rope ladders were slung over the side and they all

managed, some only just, to get aboard. Nine diggers were missing—or should I say, missed the boat in Honolulu.

After four days in Wellington, New Zealand, where the Kiwis treated us with great hospitality, we were finally on the last leg for home.

Everybody was up before dawn for the first glimpse of Australia and the cheers and whistles as we passed through the Heads gave me goose pimples. Sydney Harbour never looked so beautiful. So beautiful, in fact, that it brought tears to the eyes of many so-called tough Aussie servicemen.

We were taken by bus to Bradfield Park where our families were waiting. Mum and Dad were quick to spot me. They called out and ran across the parade ground towards me, then we hugged and kissed. It was great to see them.

'Welcome home, Vince. Thank God you're safe.'

They got us through pay parade pretty quickly. The paymaster was counting out my money. 'The five pounds you were advanced in Honolulu has been deducted from your leave pay. Actually, Flying Officer Ball, you arrived

back in Australia owing the Air Force five pounds.'

'Yer kiddin'?'

'No, Flying Officer, I am not kidding. It's all in your pay book. Check it.'

Bloody marvellous. I'm away for four years, a lot of the time fighting the Hun and I come back owing the Air Force five pounds!

My first day at home was spent talking and looking. Me looking at the family and the family looking at me. Trying, I suppose, to make up for about four years of separation. I saw big changes in my brothers and sisters, small ones in Mum and Dad. I reckon they must've noticed a big change in me ... I went away a lean eighteen year old and came back a fat fourteen and a half stone twenty-two year old.

I found it strange listening to the family and for the first time noticing their Aussie accent. Before I went overseas, I wasn't aware that we had an accent; I never thought about it. The Yanks and the Poms spoke differently, that's all. But after being surrounded by Irish, Scots, Welsh and English dialects and intonations, the Aussie voice seemed flat and nasal.

I tried telling them about the war but all I

came up with was a long travelogue, a sort of four-year holiday.

'But what about the fightin' and the flyin'?' asked Dad, who sat there puffing away at his pipe as I'd always remembered him. He had fought in World War One with the Light Horse in North Africa and then went on to Gallipoli and France and had actually seen and killed Germans and been wounded. Now that his son was home, he was waiting to hear all the gory details of war.

'There's nothin' much to tell, Dad. Yer never see the enemy. They fire at yer and yer drop bombs and depth charges and fire at them. If they hit yer, most times that's it but if yer lucky like me and lots of others, yer live to tell the tale as I'm tryin' to do now. And yer get so used to flyin', it's not a big deal any more. Our feelin' was yer can't do anythin' about it anyway. If you're number's up, that's it.'

Dad nodded, puffed away at his pipe and said, 'Your mother had an odd experience one afternoon. Tell him about it, Beez.'

Mum laughed ... how I'd missed that laugh ... and said, 'Oh, it seems silly now but I was always thinking about you and praying for

you and this one afternoon when I was doing the washing, I very clearly heard you calling me. It was coming from the loquat tree at the side of the house. I knew I was imagining things but I could still hear you calling and calling "Mum! Mum!" ever so clearly. Anyway, it sounds silly now but I rushed out to the loquat tree and of course you weren't there. It was my imagination playing tricks on me. You must think I'm mad but I wrote the date down on the calender, I'll get it.

'It was the afternoon of the third of February 1945,' she said, looking at the calendar.

Sorting out my gear that night, I came across my logbook and out of curiosity, flicked through the pages and there it was:

T/O 3/2/'45. 22.45hrs
Baltic Sea. Off Danzig. Attacked U-boats, 3 escorts and a Destroyer. Heavy flak. Captain awarded D.F.C.

We would have been off Danzig between 0200 and 0300 on 4 February 1945. Allow for the time difference—afternoon in Australia, 3 February 1945.

It was strange being back home. I loved being with the family but after a couple of days I was missing my mates. It seems everybody was feeling the same way, Nig, Johnny, Bottle.

We met in town and did a pub crawl. And that's how it was for the most part of our leave.

The Yanks dropped a couple of atom bombs on Japan and the war came to an end—something to really celebrate. By this time Jonesy and Bruce had returned so we had more celebrations.

'Would you like to take 120 airmen to Japan?' asked the Squadron Leader. 'You'd be officer-in-charge.'

'No thank you, sir, I've just come back from overseas.'

'Have you ever thought of joining the permanent Air Force, Flying Officer?'

'No sir. I would just like to get *out* of the Air Force, sir.'

'I see. We've had a request for your early release from your old firm AGE.'

So it was back to work. They were pretty good to me at AGE. 'If you get bored take the day off,' they said.

I was averaging two days off a week. I was bored out of my mind. I still had this dream of being a cowboy on the films, and by now I knew that you had to learn to be an actor. I told Mum of my ambitions.

'Don't tell anybody, Mum. They'll think I'm a bit of a sis. I'm gunna try to get into an actin' school. I've got an audition next week at 2UW for the Whitehall Academy of Dramatic Art. I'm doin' some Shakespeare.'

'Shakespeare? Oh, doesn't that sound grand. I won't tell anybody, Vince. It'll be nice to have an actor in the family. Fancy, you doing Shakespeare!'

'*Oh for a muse of fire, that would ascend the brightest heaven of invention,*
A kingdom for a stage, princes to act,
And monarchs to behold the swelling scene!'

I knew I was going too fast but somehow I couldn't stop myself. I was like a runaway train going downhill. Out of the corner of my eye I could see the people in the control room doubled over with laughter. Their bodies and open mouths playing an awful mime at my expense. The smug bastards.

'But pardon, gentles all,
The flat unraised spirits that hath dared
On this unworthy scaffold to bring forth so great
an object.'

I was doing my best. I knew nothing about Shakespeare or how it should be read but I didn't have any choice.

'A speech from any of Shakespeare's plays, no longer than three minutes.' Those were the instructions for the audition being held at radio station 2UW.

'Piece out our imperfections with your thoughts:
Into a thousand parts divide one man, and make imaginary puissance.'

That *puissance* really brought the house down. My pronunciation and strange accent, a mixture of Cockney, Canadian and Aussie, no doubt helped.

All I wanted was to be a cowboy on the films. But I had to learn how to act, and here I was taking this terrible audition which, if I passed, would get me an ex-serviceman's grant for the Whitehall Academy of Dramatic Art. *'For the which supply, admit me chorus to this history,*

Who Prologue-like your humble patience pray,
Gently to hear, kindly to judge, our play.'

Boy, the relief! It was all over. I was sweating, angry, red-faced and shaking.

'Why do you want to be an actor?' a very chi-chi voice asked over the amplifier.

'I want to be a cowboy on the fillums,' I said.

There was a dead silence. The three of them just looked at me for what seemed hours.

'Don't you want to play Romeo or Hamlet?'

'No,' I said. 'I just want to be a cowboy on the fillums and if I can act, I'll stand a better chance of makin' it.'

Silence. They stared at me.

'Can you ride a horse?'

'Yeah.'

'Okay,' the one in the middle said. 'You've passed! We'll be in touch.'

They didn't even bother to come out from that control room to say goodbye, thank you or just to wish me luck. The smug bastards. I wondered as I left if all show people were like that.

Three days later I received the letter saying that I'd been accepted and that my fees would

be paid by a government grant. The course would be for eighteen months.

It was 1946 and at last I was on my way to being an actor, with the hope that one day I would be a cowboy on the films.

That bloody war had held things up a bit. I was already twenty-two and the way things were going I could end up being the oldest sheriff in the movies.

nine

A Sibilant 'S', a Thick Lazy Tongue and the Yarrawonga

'Every time we speak, *we use our tongue and our teeth we do ... our tongue and our teeth and our lips we do ... Every time we speak the whole day through we use our tongue and our teeth and our lips we do.*'

'Now, once again.'

We did it once again.

'Well, the girls aren't so bad but I am impressed that the men can actually speak without moving their lips. Amazing!'

Our teacher, Miss Parry, had spent the first half hour of the lesson teaching us how to breathe. Apparently I had been doing it all wrong for the past twenty-two years. She said I wasn't using my diaphragm—I think that's the solar plexis.

It was my first lesson at the Whitehall Academy of Dramatic Art and I wasn't doing

very well at all, especially when we got to the reading bit. It was Shakespeare, which I didn't understand and found extremely difficult to read. My bit had a lot of S's and words like 'sufficeth'. I really made a mess of it, some words I couldn't pronounce at all. It was all very embarrassing.

Miss Parry said I had a lisp and a sibilant 'S' which made things difficult for me. She said she would give me some exercises to practise.

'Also Vincent, try to remember that there is a "G" at the end of all the "ings". Hunt*ing* —fish*ing*—shoot*ing*. Not huntin'—fishin'— shootin'. Alright?

'Also, it's: "I picked up *my* hat and *my* coat and said, 'I'll see *you* all later'." Not, "I picked up *me* hat and *me* coat and said 'I'll see *yer* all later'." Alright, Vincent? You must try to be grammatical.'

'Yes, Miss Parry.'

'The exercises I have given you all tonight, you must practise. *Practise, practise, practise*! In the trams, buses, trains, everywhere. Don't worry about people staring at you. Use your lips and your teeth and your tongue, open your mouth, drop your jaw. Read the advertisements

that you see on the billboards—*out aloud*. You must aim for good diction, flexibility, articulation and resonance.'

All the way home on the train from Town Hall to Epping I struggled with one of the exercises I'd been given: 'The Leith Police dismisseth us.'

As I walked through the darkened streets of Epping, I thought I'd give it a go and try it out loud.

The Leith Perlice dismisseth thus.

The Leith Po-lice dismitheth uth.

The Leith Po-lice dismitheth uth us.

Bloody hell. I was slowly realising that I couldn't talk properly. The only way I could do it was unnatural. I had to sort of spell it out. Well, it was much easier to say, 'Don't make a move. Go fer yer gun and yer a dead man.'

'Whoa Silver, steady boy.'

Even so, you couldn't have a cowboy hero with a lisp and a sibilant 'S'. Nobody would take you seriously and besides, people might get the wrong idea.

I gave up my job at AGE. I was working at their factory at Villawood and I found it too much trouble getting into town two nights one

The girl that I married. Her name's Doreen.

The Old Rectory (from the front).

The Old Rectory (from the side).

The family at the Old Rectory, 1962.

ABOVE: Ernest Borgnine, Johnny Mills and me in *The Summer of the Seventeenth Doll.*

BELOW: Al Garcia, Frank Wilson, Deryck Barnes and me in *The Summer of the Seventeenth Doll.*

You'll notice all my team are smiling. It was a good lunch.
BACK ROW: Donald Houston (second from left), Vic Friendly
(fourth from left), next to him Don Chaffey and Chris Jamieson.
CENTRE (LEFT TO RIGHT): Leo McKern, Les Leston, unknown,
John Meillon, Ed Deveraux. *FRONT ROW:* Harold Jamieson, me.

After another long lunch my team take the field, only slightly
the worse for wear. *LEFT TO RIGHT:* Donald Houston, Vic Friendly
(behind), Don Chaffey. *RIGHT TO LEFT:* Les Leston, me, Chris
Jamieson, Leo McKern (at the back).

ABOVE: Me and Davy Crockett (Fess Parker), Junior Television.

BELOW: Victor Maddern, me and Sir Donald Wolfit in *Blood of the Vampire.*

The closest I ever got to being a cowboy.
Me as Sergeant Garland in *Ben Hall*.

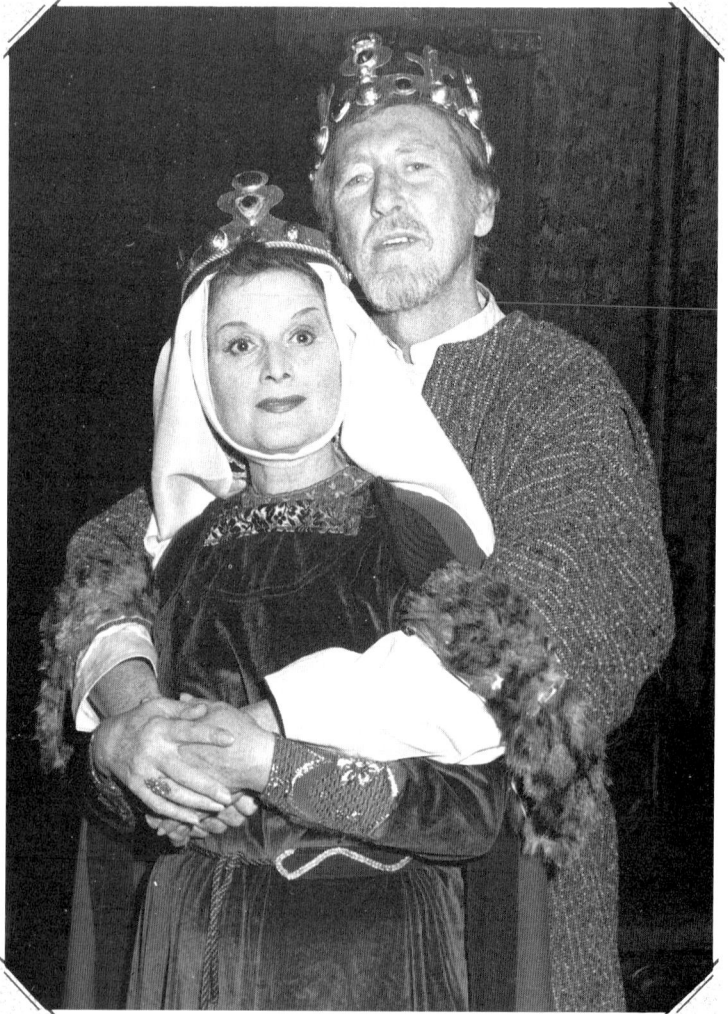

Doreen and me in *The Lion in Winter* at the Bondi Pavilion.

week, then one night the following week and trying to fit in Rugby training twice a week at Eastwood. Instead, I took up a job as the assistant paymaster at the Crown Street Women's Hospital.

' "Are you copper bottoming 'em?"
"No, I'm aluminiuming 'em Mum".'

That was my exercise for the day. I'd been trying to master one exercise a day but I'd been on this one for two days already and I still couldn't do it at a natural speed.

The lady on the train in the seat opposite had given up reading the paper and so had a few others. They just sat there watching me squirming, pulling faces and mouthing words trying to get that sentence right. I'm sure they were willing me on, I don't suppose they could stand another day of it.

' "Are you copper bottominging 'em 'em?"
"No, I'm aluminiming 'em Mum".'

Aw shit.

At the end of the first term I came second last, the only person I beat was a wharfie, Don, a nice bloke. I beat him by one mark.

Whenever I travelled to Wynyard and walked down the steps to the exits, I could see

this big advertisement up on the wall in front of me: DID YOU PROTEX YOURSELF THIS MORNING?

And I used to practise saying it softly all the way down the steps. I got some funny looks but I didn't mind at all; I was determined to speak 'proper'. I must admit, I did get one very positive reaction from an attractive blonde who said quietly in my ear, 'Yes, as a matter of fact, I did.' And she gave me a very strange old look.

'Where do you go at nights, Snow?'

I was in the changing shed getting ready for Rugby training. 'I ... er ... go to tech. Studying accountancy.'

'Yer speak a bit funny now. What are you doin' that for? Yer sound a bit poofy sometimes.'

He was a big front-row forward so I didn't argue.

'No, it's ... er ... y'see ... I've got a bit of a ... er ... sibilant "S" problem and I'm just trying to correct it. That's all.'

'Aw ... gee ... Sibilant "S", eh? Sorry about that.' He made it sound like a disease.

Well, I suppose I did sound a bit strange. I was in such a state about my speech, my

grammar, my consonants, my vowels, my every-thing! It seems nothing was right. I'd reached the stage where I was frightened to speak; it was an effort to open my mouth. I'd never realised how difficult it was to talk properly. Well, not until I went to the Whitehall Academy of Dramatic Art.

My lisp and sibilant 'S' took over my life. Every word seemed to be fill of TH's and S's. Trying to say a simple word like 'sympathy' was a nightmare and 'sufficeth' was an impossible dream. Practise, practise, practise. I became an oddity on the trams and trains of Sydney, but even-tually, I say eventually, I could more or less say, 'The Leith Police dismisseth us' without making a complete charlie of myself. I became a good lis-tener and not much of a talker, for obvious reasons, and took to nodding and smiling a lot. Amongst the acting crowd I got the reputation of being a shy, quiet sort of bloke, and on top of all that Miss Parry, our voice teacher, then told me I had a thick lazy tongue. Bloody hell, a thick lazy tongue as well! And that I had a language all of my own, made up of words like, gunna, sorta, kinda, yer, jus' and 'em.

'Think before you speak and sound your consonants,' she said.

Being an aspiring actor makes you aware of your true physical appearance. It had never bothered me before, I'd always thought that I was a fairly presentable sort of bloke, but now it turns out that I'm built like a duck—close to the ground, long neck and body, short legs, a big bum and I'm bandy as well!

I kept seeing this lisping, short-legged, bandy sheriff, facing the town bully on Main Street. Not a pretty sight. I spent a lot of time at the pictures checking to see if the western heroes had bandy legs. It was all too depressing. Most of them stood tall and straight.

By now I had so many hang-ups it wasn't true. And when I think back to that interview for my commission in the Air Force and the question about rabbits and how I told them that we were, 'shootin' 'em, poisonin' em, gassin' 'em and trappin' 'em.' Not a 'G' or 'TH' in sight. What must they have thought. Officer material? I've often wondered what was in that letter from the education officer?

Eventually my secret was out and I took a lot of good-natured ribbing, even on the field. Some of the team would put on a posh Pommy voice and say things like, 'Give it to Snow,

there's a good chap,' and 'Well done, Snow old boy!' and 'Oh, jolly good show, old boy.'

All of them elocuting like mad.

'My name's Bill Redmond. I saw your scene at the end of your first term. You need elocution and voice production lessons. I'd like to help.'

'Yeah, well that's kind of you Bill, the classes I have here and the practise I do don't seem to be enough. I dunno whether I'm doin' it right or not. I'm finding it pretty hard.'

'That's because you don't breathe properly and you don't open your mouth. There's an English girl in my class who is a qualified elocution teacher. She saw your scene too. She could help you, so I'll introduce you if you like? Her reaction to your scene was that you should stick to Rugby or farming.'

Well, that sounds like a pretty good start!

A couple of nights later he introduced us.

'This is Doreen Harrop . . . Vincent Ball.'

'Hello. Nice to meet you,' she said.

'Hello.'

She wasn't a bad-looking sort. Lovely English voice.

'Bill said you may be able to give me a bit

of a hand with my voice. I seem to do everything wrong.'

'Let's talk about it after classes. We go to Repins for coffee, why don't you join us?'

I was right out of my depth. Doreen was in the senior class at the Academy and they all seemed to know about Shakespeare and characters and plays and they all chatted away like mad. I couldn't join in because I didn't know enough about what they were talking about and anyway I couldn't express myself that well. I thought that what a couple of them had to say was a load of bullshit though.

'What do *you* think, Vincent?'

'Ah ... I ... er ... agree with you, Doreen. Yes, I agree with you.'

'You see, Bill? I'm right. Vincent backs me up.'

I really didn't have a clue what they were talking about.

Playing Rugby for Eastwood and trying to become an actor didn't seem to be working out too well. I broke my right thumb in the match against Drummoyne and what with the bandages and splints, my thumb became very big and

stuck straight up. I was playing the clerk of the court from the trial scene in *The Merchant of Venice* and Doreen was playing Portia. Mr Blackman, the producer, thought my upright thumb would distract the audience from the 'Quality of Mercy' speech.

'Vince, old man. Try to keep the right hand out of sight. It looks positively obscene.'

Doreen and I had been going out together for some time now. We enjoyed each other's company and my interest in cowboys was waning a bit. Now I just wanted to be a good actor. She was a great help to me, hearing my lines, telling and showing me how to say them. And she had the added advantage of living at Bondi, a few hundred yards from the beach.

Maybe Doreen's first reaction to seeing me act was right, maybe I should stick to farming or Rugby. I was waiting in the wings ready to make my entrance, trying to remember my first line. I was playing the lead in a student production of *Hippolytus*, a Greek play by Euripides, at the Minerva Theatre.

I had gold dust in my hair, a gold band around my head, was wearing a short toga and

sandals with gold leather straps criss-crossed up to my knees, carrying a wreath of flowers ... and half the Rugby team were out front. I was petrified. My mouth was so dry that my tongue could hardly move.

I made my entrance, walked to the centre of the stage, knelt down on one knee, raised the wreath of flowers to the Gods and said, 'To thee this wreathed garland from a green and virgin land bear I, Oh my Queen.'

An audible whisper came from the audience, 'Good on yer, Snow!'

Shit. That's all I need ... audience participation.

Apart from that slight pause, I managed to get through the whole play without 'drying'. Which I thought wasn't bad because most of the time I didn't really know what the hell I was talking about. Doreen said I was improving.

All the footy team wanted to know was whether I was wearing anything under my toga and who was the big blonde in the front of the chorus?

Doreen finished the course and was put under contract by the Minerva Theatre. They really got their money's worth from her. She was

playing Peter in *Peter Pan* during the day, sometimes for two performances, and appearing in *Life with Father* at night.

She made a lovely Peter, I was really proud of her. Well, why shouldn't I be? She was my girl.

Here we go again. Waiting in the wings, wishing I had taken up farming or anything but acting. Dry lips, tongue stuck to the roof of my mouth, worried about my sibilant 'S' and petrified with stage fright. It was my final piece at the Academy and I was doing the 'banishment' scene from *Romeo and Juliet*.

Doreen had talked me into having a dark rinse in my hair, darkened eyebrows, mascara on my eyelashes—the lot. I looked like the Italian who sold me fruit at the Epping greengrocers.

The chap playing Friar Lawrence seemed to be having problems too. He'd developed a slight tic in his right eye. What a pair!

Buck Jones, where are you?

I was going like a bomb. I'd forgotten about my stage fright and was right into it. I'd done most of the big speeches and hadn't lisped once.

FRIAR: Thou fond mad man, hear me a little speak.

ROMEO: O, thou wilt speak again of banishment.

FRIAR: I'll give thee armour to keep off that word;
Adversity's sweet milk, philosophy,
To comfort thee, though thou art banished.

ROMEO: Yet 'banished' . . .?

I must have moved too violently on 'banished' because my dagger slipped out of the small scabbard, fell to the floor and broke in two. It was a stage dagger—a hilt glued to a blade. Bugger it, I couldn't take my eyes off the broken dagger. How was I going to look as if I was about to stab myself at the end of the scene?

FRIAR: Arise, one knocks. Good Romeo, hide thyself.

All through the scene between the Friar and the Nurse, I was trying to figure out how to pick up that dagger. With a bit of luck, I might be able to do it in one movement.

ROMEO: O, tell me, friar, tell me,
In what vile part of this anatomy
Doth my name lodge?
Tell me that I may sack
The hateful mansion.

And in one swoop, I smoothly picked up both pieces and held the dagger above my head. Aw shit.

The hilt was pointing towards me and the blade was between my fingers pointing in a different direction and no matter how I contorted my hand and body, I couldn't get that bloody blade to point towards me ...

FRIAR: Hold thy desperate hand.

There was a long pause ... The Friar seemed fascinated by the dagger. All through his speech he held my wrist and I noticed his tic had come back.

I was given a certificate saying that I had attended the Drama Course at the Whitehall Academy of Dramatic Art, graduating in 1947.

The Rank Organisation at Pinewood Studios in

England was looking for a fair-haired young actor who could swim, to play opposite Jean Simmons in a film called *The Blue Lagoon*. The *Sydney Morning Herald* said that the director, Frank Launder, had been conducting a world-wide search for someone suitable for the part. I rang Doreen and told her about it.

'Why don't you get some photographs done and send them off. You're a good swimmer. You never know.'

I went to Noel Rubie, the photographer, covered my body with oil, flexed what muscles I had, pulled my gut in and struck several poses. Doreen helped me with the letter and off it went with the photos to Pinewood Studios. I never really expected to hear about it again.

About three weeks later, I received a letter.

'Yes, we will consider you for the part but you're 13,000 miles away. If you ever should be around this way, do come and see us.' As though it was just around the corner.

That was good enough for me—but how to get to England? I didn't have any money; Doreen and I had taken care of most of my deferred Air Force pay at various nightclubs around Sydney and Randwick racecourse had seen to the rest.

The next couple of weeks were spent trudging around the docks of Sydney Harbour trying to find a job on a ship going to England.

Luck was on my side. A Swedish cargo-boat, the *Yarrawonga*, offered me the 'position' of dishwasher and deck-scraper for the princely sum of 8 pounds a month all found. I jumped at it. And pretty soon I set sail for England, fame and fortune, thinking I'd be there in about six weeks.

Six months later, I arrived in Sweden.

The *Yarrawonga* was a sort of tramp steamer. We started off in Sydney, then on to Melbourne and Hobart and back again to Sydney where I had to say all those goodbyes again. Then off to Melbourne once more and from there to Port Pirie where there was a dock strike so we spent a couple of weeks shark-fishing in the Bight—using legs of lamb for bait. On to Fremantle, then across the Indian Ocean to Aden, where the steward and I, with the help of Gordons Gin, managed to miss the boat.

We got the ship's agent to radio the *Yarrawonga*, but the captain was so angry he said he would slow down but wouldn't stop.

We offered an Arab, the owner of a small

motorboat, everything we had—including the clothes we stood up in—if he could catch the *Yarrawonga*. And catch it he did ... in the Red Sea. We clambered up a rope ladder in our underpants, to the ironic cheers of the crew.

The steward was fined and hauled over the coals for leading me astray!

This business about sailors loving the sea was a load of rubbish. All they ever did was look forward to the next port and the entertainment it provided. It would take them about three days to recover from the ordeal and then they'd start thinking about the next port of call.

We sailed through the Suez Canal to Port Said where a 'wily oriental gentleman' sold me a large bottle of White Horse whisky. I'd been warned about these bottles of 'whisky'. I looked at that bottle for about ten minutes. The seal was intact; everything about it was right. They can't fool me, so I bought it. And of course it was tea!

When we reached Haifa I became involved in another war, this time between the Arabs and the Jews. Lying in my bunk at night I could hear the bullets hitting the side of the ship.

The Jews and the Arabs would work together all day unloading the cargo, with the

Arabs 'accidentally' dropping the odd case of tinned fruit. The speed with which two dozen cans could disappear into the folds of their robes was amazing! Then they'd go home, have a bite to eat, get their guns out and fire off about 30,000 rounds at each other—and all be back the next day, minus one or two, working together on the dock.

A week in Beirut—a wide, open port that satisfied the tastes of all members of the crew, which was made up of Swedes, Finns, Germans, Norwegians, Danes, and Australians. Held up in Marseilles for three weeks—another strike. Would I ever get to England?

I'd been at sea for about four months already and I was practically through *The Outline of Literature*, the book Doreen had given to me to improve my mind. It weighed a ton. I don't know what it is but I seem to present some sort of challenge to people because so many want to educate me or improve my mind. Maybe they're just being helpful.

'Vincent Ball?'

'Yes.'

We were docked at Newcastle-upon-Tyne.

'Anything to declare?' asked the Customs officer as he stepped into my cabin.

'Not really. Half a bottle of Scotch, nearly a carton of cigarettes.'

'Nothing else?'

'No.'

Without saying another word he pulled out a screwdriver, unfolded the small stepladder he was carrying and simply unscrewed the wooden battens covering the electric wires in the cabin—then emptied 5000 cigarettes into his little black bag.

'Do you know anything about these?'

'No, I don't. I had no idea they were there. I wish I *had* known. I'd have taken them. How long do you think they've been there?'

'Oh, I'd say about a day. I wonder why,' giving me an odd look, 'they always put them there? So obvious. Good morning.'

Strewth. And I thought I was being so smart ... but he didn't find the ones buried at the bottom of the big sugar bin. That corny old saying is right, 'Win a few, lose a few.'

I had decided to go on to Sweden. The captain had invited me to stay with him and his family, and the first engineer, with whom I had

consumed many a bottle of Aquavi't, had done the same.

'Wincent, the captain wants to see you on the bridge.'

'The crew have offered to pay for you to stay for two weeks at a hotel in Goteborg. It's a form of repayment for all the letters you wrote for them and, as far as I'm concerned, for being a stand-by radio operator.'

It was an offer I couldn't refuse.

'You must write very good letters?'

'Er . . . yes, sir . . . er . . . thank you, sir.'

Those letters or should I say love letters had got out of hand. On the way out from Sweden, the crew of the *Yarrawonga* had made friends with girls in every port in Australia and, of course, had somehow promised to write, see them on the way back and God knows what else. But quite a few couldn't speak English, let alone write it.

It had all started when we were between Sydney and Melbourne for the second time. I was sitting on deck writing a letter to Mum, when Sven approached me. You could say that Sven and I were on good nodding terms. Every time we passed each other, he would nod and smile and say something in Swedish and I would

nod and smile and say, 'Good morning', 'Good evening' or 'G'day'.

'Wincent … Me Sven. Write letter … Say … meet … boat Fremantle. Ya?' he asked, shoving a greasy bit of paper under my nose.

'Sven. I am Vincent. See?' writing 'VINCENT' on the back of the pad. 'VIN-CENT'.

'Ya,' said Sven looking at it and smiling, 'Wincent!'

It seems the Swedes pronounce W's for V's.

'Love … Me,' he said, tapping his chest. 'Love,' tapping the piece of paper that had a name and address on it.

'Sven, you love her?'

'Ya. Ya,' said the dark-haired electrician. Not all Swedes are blond.

'Do you want to marry her?'

'Nay, nay! Meet *Yarrawonga* … Fremantle … you say … Nice things … for me. Ya?'

'Me write love letter for you?'

'Ya, ya. You … make … love … letter … for … me.'

'I'll try, Sven. Okay?'

'Okay, Wincent. Tac tac,' and he wandered off.

Bloody hell! Write a love letter for a non-English speaking Swede?

Yarrawonga,
At Sea

Dearest Ruby,

I am writing this letter for Sven who is standing beside me and telling me in broken English and gestures more or less what to say. These are his words, Ruby, not mine. I am just putting them together for him.

Sven says that for him time has stood still since your last meeting and that the days and nights, especially the nights, are empty without the touch of your soft, gentle hands on his flesh and the subtle fragrance of your perfume.

He says he knew he was in love when he watched Fremantle fade into the distance and had the overwhelming urge to jump overboard and swim back to you.

My darling, I count the hours and minutes until I am in your arms once more.

Ruby my love, I am working hard on my English so that soon, very soon, I can write my own loving letters to you, my darling.

Goodbye my dearest,
Until we meet in Fremantle,
Lots and lots of love,
Sven.

PS Check the shipping list in the paper for our exact date of arrival.

'My name Carl, Wincent. You write letter for me too? To Port Pirie. Ya?'

'Ya, Carl. Okay. Got the name and address?'

'Ya,' handing me the back of a cigarette packet.

'Do you love her, Carl?'

'Ya, ya.'

'But you don't want to marry her?'

'Nay, nay.'

'But you want,' looking at the name, 'Betty to meet the *Yarrawonga*, ya?'

'Ya. Tac tac, Wincent.'

'Okay. I'll give it to you soon.'

Strike a light, that's the fourth one since I got the steward to read my letter to Sven in Swedish. Obviously, the whole crew aft had listened too. So far, two for Port Pirie, two for Fremantle.

As I left the bridge, I mentally thanked Ruby, Betty, Raelene, Jill, Helen, and the others for the good time they obviously gave the crew members

who were now thanking me with two weeks' holiday in Goteborg. And what a two weeks it was!

I think every Swedish member of the crew sent young 'lady friends' to show me the sights and to make sure I wasn't bored.

When I left, they presented me with a grey double-breasted suit made of wood pulp. It was a bit of a worry, I thought, when people were lighting cigarettes near me.

I travelled steerage to England on the *Saga*, a small Swedish passenger ship. The cabin that I shared with three other chaps was so far below the waterline that we were level with the propeller. Its constant hum and the vibrations of the driving shaft made sure I had a sleepless passage to my new home.

ten

KEEP YOUR FACE AWAY
FROM THE CAMERA OLD BOY

AT LAST I WAS IN England to start my career as an actor. I stood on Charing Cross Station with my officer's tin trunk and ten pounds in my pocket.

By eight o'clock the following morning I had agreed over the phone to take a bed-sitter in Elsworthy Terrace, Swiss Cottage, for two pounds a week.

'You catch the tube to Uxbridge and then a bus that drops you right at the gates of Pinewood Studios.'

'Thank you. That's very kind of you.'

What a nice receptionist. It was good to be back in England.

I opened the envelope and pulled out a very grubby beer-stained letter that had been shown to drinking mates in various dockside pubs

around the world, and gave it to the man on the gate at Pinewood Studios. He read it, looked at me for a bit and then picked up the phone.

I was taken to the main building, up the steps that were guarded by two large stone lions, and shown into an office.

'My name is Denis Van Thal, and this is Derek Marr. Our names are on this letter that we wrote you. I'm terribly sorry but we've more or less finished the film, been to Fiji and back again ... but ... er ... we do have a problem. Donald Houston who plays the lead can't swim.'

'He can't swim?'

'That's right. Can you?'

'What?'

'Swim.'

'I'm an Australian.'

'Yes, of course. Would you like to double for him? Do some of the underwater swimming? We would pay you ten pounds a day.'

Ten pounds a day! That sounded like a fortune. Anyway it was five weeks' rent.

'Yes, I'll do it. When do I start?'

'The day after tomorrow.'

For two days I wrestled a rubber octopus made by Dunlops, cut shells off rocks and

generally swam around in a freezing tank at Pinewood. Apparently they couldn't heat the water because it affected the filming, making it cloudy. Another actor/swimmer, Neil Hallet, was more or less doing the same.

Every time we came out of the water we were given a brandy while standing in front of a hot fan, so by the end of the day we were slightly pissed.

'Vince, old man. Try to keep your face away from the camera. There's a good chap.'

'Yes, Mr Launder.'

What a great start to my film career!

At the end of the second day, they paid me twenty pounds. Ten weeks' rent; I could only think in terms of rent.

'Vincent, we have a school, it's closing in two weeks but I wondered if you'd like to go for that time. We'll pay you five pounds a week expenses. It'll help out a bit.'

Denis Van Thal, I think, felt responsible for me because it was his letter that had brought me halfway across the world. So I went to what was known as 'The Rank Charm School' where I spent most of my time fencing with Anthony Steel and Bill Travers.

I also met a rather attractive blonde starlet by the name of Sandra Dorne who introduced me to her agent, Gee Martin, who agreed to handle me. Apart from being my agent, Gee was also the owner of the Norfolk Hotel in Paddington and sensing my financial situation offered me a job. I shall always be grateful to her—a caring, generous friend.

In return for free room and board, I was to look after the boiler in the hotel and be on call to let rooms at night. My room was in the basement next to the boiler and one of the smallest I'd ever seen. If I leant out the window, it was like looking up a lift well, except that I could see a square of sky at the top, and that was the situation when Doreen arrived from Sarawak.

Things weren't too good between Doreen and me. I'd written to her while on the *Yarrawonga* more or less breaking off our relationship, saying that I was too young, that being an actor was too precarious, I had nothing to offer her and I didn't want to muck up her life, etc, etc.

Doreen had written back saying, if that's the way I felt, so be it, but would I find a room for her to rent in London. She would be arriving on

14 October. She said it wasn't necessary for me to meet her on arrival, just leave the address of the room with the P&O Line and they'd see that she got it.

Well I must admit I nearly chickened out, but what kind of bastard would I be to let her arrive, a stranger in London, with nobody to meet her. I hadn't any idea where she wanted to live or what rent she was prepared to pay, so I booked her into one of the cheaper single rooms at the Norfolk Hotel for a week and then she could find her own accommodation.

I nervously watched the boat train pull into Charing Cross Station and start to disgorge its passengers. Then I saw her, right at the end of the platform.

She stood there, straight backed, head proudly held high, a perky little hat on her perky little head, looking like a million dollars. As I walked towards her, I thought I must be crazy to even think of losing her.

She saw me, raised her chin a little higher and waited, not moving; making me walk the whole length of the platform. It was like some sort of challenge, like walking down the main

street at noon after being called out by the town bully. Except that instead of being cool, being the fastest gun in the West, I was tripping over my feet. Why was I so bloody nervous?

'Hello, how are you,' she said cheerfully. Too cheerfully, I thought.

'I'm ... er ... fine ... er ... did you have a good trip?'

'Absolutely marvellous.'

Just then a chap of about thirty-something came up and held out his hand to Doreen saying, 'Don't forget. Any problems, give me a ring,' eyeing me up and down.

We caught a taxi from Charing Cross to the hotel. Doreen kept up a constant stream of chatter and she was so bloody cheerful with it, no mention of our 'finished' relationship. It was all about her trip and the nice rubber-planter, Andrew, she had met.

Gee had prepared lunch for us and she and the staff welcomed Doreen like a long lost daughter. I was pretty well ignored, all I got were sidelong glances. I was bloody glad when the meal was over.

I wonder if Doreen would take me back? She didn't seem to care about the letter I had

written her, she was so cheerful ... maybe that was why she was so bloody cheerful. I knew that being an actor was going to be rough but we were young and together we could make a go of it, and if I did go to Hollywood to try to be a cowboy on the films, she'd come with me. At least we'd have each other—I wonder if she'd have me back?

I tapped on her door. 'It's me ... er ... I ... er wonder if you'd like to come for a walk through Hyde Park? We could go up to Marble Arch and Speakers Corner?'

'Love to. I'm changing, be out in a minute.'

It was a beautiful autumn day. The sun was shining, families were out walking, dogs were barking, children were playing and I was trying to pluck up enough courage to talk about our relationship. Why didn't *she* say something about it?

'Doreen ... er ... when I wrote, you know, that letter from the *Yarrawonga*, I meant what I said ... er ... at the time but I was a bit mixed up and since then I realise I was wrong and since seeing you again I ... er ... know I made a mistake and I wondered if you'd give me ... er ... you know ... er ... another chance,

if we could try again. I've missed you.'

Doreen looked at me for a bit. Well quite a long time really. 'Of course darling.'

I had noticed that she was wearing a pearl ring on her right hand; two lovely pearls mounted on a gold band.

'That's a nice ring.'

'Yes. Mummy gave it to me.'

'I'll buy it off you for a shilling.'

'Alright.'

I fished out a shilling and gave it to her. She held out her right hand. I slipped the ring off her finger, lifted her left hand and put the ring on her engagement finger.

'Do you mind?'

'No I don't mind. Oh darling how romantic.' And we walked happily, hand-in-hand, towards Marble Arch.

My career seemed to be on hold at this particular time, 1948, but at least I had Doreen with me and the boiler at the hotel and I had reached a truce. I know actors can be temperamental but they had nothing on this coke-spitting bloody boiler. For the first few weeks my relationship with this iron monster was fraught to say the least. My ambition changed

from wanting to be a cowboy on the films to keeping this boiler going twenty-four hours a day. We now had a working arrangement, which enabled me to spend the day away from the hotel knowing that when I returned it would still be alight. To pay my way I was also helping out at my agent's office, a sort of general dogsbody for two or three afternoons a week.

Things looked like they were about to take a turn for the better when Gee said that Mr X wanted to see me. Mr X was a big impresario in London's West End, a distinguished-looking gentleman who had his offices in the same building as hers. I'd often passed him on the stairs and found him to be a friendly sort of bloke who always said hello.

Doreen and I were very excited about the interview. Maybe it was just the break I was looking for.

I was shown into Mr X's office. He rose from behind a large desk, indicating a chair. 'Sit down, Vincent.'

I sat down.

'I'll get straight to the point,' he said. 'I'm in love with you.'

Bloody hell! I sat, frozen, unable to speak, staring at this very distinguished man who'd just told me he loved me.

'I had to get it off my chest and tell you. I've often seen you in the building and it's no good keeping it to myself. I have to know if maybe there's a chance that you could, in time, possibly feel the same way. Not now, of course, but in the future.'

I was still staring at him—it was like some sort of dream. How often does an aspiring actor get a proposal of marriage from a charming male impresario? My mouth must have been opening and closing . . .

'Before you say anything, let me finish my proposal. I would want you to live with me in my Mayfair house. You would be seen at all the best places, attend first nights and premieres, your clothes would come from Saville Row. I will have you coached in Dramatic Art and when a suitable role comes along I would do my utmost to help you get it. And, of course, you would have an allowance.'

All I could think of to say was, 'I'm not like that.'

'You don't want to think about it?'

'No. My girlfriend is waiting downstairs in the coffee shop.'

He smiled and said, 'I see.' He moved over to a cocktail cabinet. 'Would you like a drink? Scotch?'

'Thank you.' God did I need a drink.

He handed me the Scotch. 'No hard feelings?'

That made me smile a bit. 'No hard feelings,' I replied.

'There is one thing I must ask of you. Of course it's your choice. That you never divulge my name when at some future date you are telling this story. I would appreciate that.'

'I promise. You have my word.'

'Thank you. Any time you want any help in the future, just pick up the phone and I'll do what I can.'

What a nice bloke, I thought.

He handed me a small card. 'I'm having a cocktail party tomorrow. Why don't you and your girlfriend come along.'

'Did you get the job darling?'

'No such luck. It was just a general interview. We've been invited to a cocktail party.'

Mr X made us most welcome at the party. Doreen was very impressed.

'What a charming man,' she said.

I suppose there were about fifty people there, mostly from the theatre and film world. Doreen and I did a lot of star spotting, eating and drinking. As we left, I looked back at the elegant room with its ornate ceiling, antique furnishings, thick carpet and thought, 'That could have all been mine.'

At this stage the nearest I got to acting were the odd day's filming for Ronnie Curtis, the casting director for the Guild House Producers, who made documentaries for the Army, Navy and Police.

It was while I was working on one of these that I met an actor named Harold Jamieson who had just finished the course at RADA—the Royal Academy of Dramatic Art. Over a few beers after filming, he suggested that I needed more experience and why didn't I try RADA.

'You're joking. I'd never get in there.'

'Well, you can try. Let's get an application form and have a go. I'll give you any help you need.'

Jamie (Harold Jamieson) and Doreen coached me day after day after day in Jamie's basement flat in Seymour Place. It was known to one and all as 'The Hovel'.

I had chosen—or I should say they had chosen for me—a piece from Emlyn William's *Light of Heart* and one of Hotspur's speeches from *Henry IV Part I*. They rehearsed me word by word, inflection by inflection and move by move. So it wasn't really me that went along for the audition but this trained parrot.

The room was full of twitchy would-be actors who all looked about sixteen and, of course, me at twenty-five with the dry lips, etc, etc.

'My name is Vincent Ball . . . *Light of Heart* by Emlyn Williams.' And off I went.

Got through that one alright, now for Hotspur.

'My liege, I did deny no prisoners . . .' I thought I was doing okay and I was about halfway through it when—

'Thank you! Thank you very much.'

Aw shit, I thought. I pushed the chair away and headed for the door.

'Where are you going?' asked the elderly gentleman.

'Well, I thought as you stopped me, that was it.'

'We would like you to come back next Thursday and try for a scholarship. Can you do that?'

'Yes, sir! Thank you, sir ... er ... everybody. Thank you.'

There were about six or eight judges. I was too nervous to count them but thought it polite to thank them all.

Try for a scholarship? That would be the answer. Because even if I did get in, how was I going to pay for it, or keep myself? Just have to work nights, I suppose.

Frederick Treves, another friend and an ex-RADA mate of Jamie's, said that Sir Kenneth Barnes, the head of the RADA, liked something religious.

So for *my* scholarship, Doreen, Jamie and Fred chose Masefield's *Good Friday* and *The Voice of the Turtle* as a contrast. The week flew by. They rehearsed me day and night, and as before I learnt it like a parrot.

'There's a bit of a party on tonight. Why don't you come along for a while. Help you to

relax for tomorrow and take your mind off the audition. We won't stay long,' said Jamie.

I just managed to get back to my room, have a bath, stoke the boiler and get to RADA in time for the audition.

I seemed very relaxed. I think I was still a bit pissed. No dry lips, no tongue stuck to the roof of my mouth ... no nothing ... and no sleep. Everybody else in the room looked a little edgy. So this very relaxed parrot went in to do his scholarship pieces.

'Vincent Ball. John Masefield's *Good Friday*.'

'*They nailed him there aloft, among the thieves in the bright air ...*'

One down. One to go.

'"Bill" in a scene from *The Voice of the Turtle*,' and off I went with my Doreen, Jamie and Fred's American accent.

'Thank you. Would you wait outside. We'll call you in later.'

Eventually I was called in and stood in front of the eight judges.

'Could you come to the Royal Academy of Dramatic Art if we gave you a scholarship?' asked Sir Kenneth Barnes.

'Yes, sir. But I'll need to have a bit of time off to earn some money to live on.'

'Don't you have any money?' he asked.

I didn't have any but I felt if I said that they might whip the hat round. And that would be too embarrassing.

'I've got eight pounds, sir. I'm working as a bricklayer's labourer, sir. Keeping two brickies going on scaffolding in Maida Vale.'

'How old are you?' asked a lady. Obviously she hadn't read my application form.

'Twenty-five, Miss . . . er . . . Madam.'

'You're much *older* than the majority of applicants.'

'Yes, well, you see I joined the RAAF when I was eighteen, trained in Canada and the Bahamas and then came over to England as a wireless air gunner on Liberator bombers and did fifty-three operational trips. Then after VE Day I went back to Australia to be involved in the Japanese war but the Americans dropped the atom bomb so I was demobbed from the Air Force and, because I'd always wanted to be a serious actor, I joined a drama school for two nights one week and one night the next. But I knew that the *only* place that

I could get the *best* training was at the Royal Academy of Dramatic Art so I spent my lunch-hours and evenings trudging around to all the docks in Sydney Harbour looking for a job on a ship going to England as I didn't have any money and the only way I could get here was by working my passage. Eventually I got a job on a Swedish cargo boat, a sort of tramp steamer, and I spent six months at sea scraping and red-leading the decks. But I got to England. And here I am. I would have been here when I was much younger but the war held me up.'

Nobody said anything for a bit, they all had this sort of glazed look on their faces. I hadn't given them a chance to interrupt.

'Yes ... er ... well, thank you. We'll be in touch,' said Sir Kenneth Barnes.

The next day I got a letter saying I had been awarded a scholarship plus five pounds a week from the Commonwealth Rhodes Trust fund.

It was during these traumatic days that I made friends with an actor, Hugh Falkus, who had been a Spitfire pilot during the Battle of Britain and to me looked every inch the part. Tall, good-looking, very English, wore suede

shoes, corduroys, a tweed jacket with leather patches, check shirt, cravat and was a huntin', shootin' and fishin' man.

Unfortunately he'd been shot down over France on his third op, and spent the rest of the war tunnelling under half of Germany in various stalags, trying to escape. He never made it, but had helped many others to get away. So when he was called to Pinewood Studios to see the producers of a true-to-life escape film that was being made, *The Wooden Horse*, he was on top of the world, because he had actually worked on the real thing and helped with the tunnelling in that particular stalag.

'They said, "I was the wrong type" old boy. They said, "I was the wrong type".' And he kept repeating it over and over until the pub closed. Doreen and I tried to ease the pain with pints of bitter but Hugh was a shattered man and would not be consoled. I think at that point he gave up acting, to eventually became a successful writer of nature books, documentaries and narrations, and from his cottage in Cumbria he teaches the finer points of trout fishing to would-be anglers.

'If you have a cigarette, a pint of beer and

a friend to drink with you're a rich man', was his favourite saying.

He christened me 'Buck Ball' after watching me rehearse my Shakespearian pieces for RADA. He said they were 'different'; my movement and delivery had a certain 'cowboyish' quality. I took it as a compliment.

'Mr Harrop, Doreen and I would like to get married sometime.'

Doreen's parents were on leave from Sarawak and had a flat near Chalk Farm.

Mrs Harrop, I think, had wanted Doreen to marry an English rubber-planter or somebody high up in the Colonial Service. She wasn't too mad about the idea of a student/actor, and an Australian to boot—especially one who was covered in cement dust. I thought if I came straight from my job with the brickies in my working clothes it would show Doreen's parents that I wasn't afraid of work or getting my hands dirty.

'You're what? Twenty-five? Quite young. Why don't you wait until our next leave in three years' time? By then you'll have finished at RADA and be settled in your career.'

'Yes, alright, Mr Harrop. Thank you.'

As their ship weighed anchor at Tilbury and everybody was frantically waving farewell, I said, 'How about we get married next week? Is that alright for you?'

'Yes, that's alright for me. Bye, Mummy! Bye, Daddy!'

Doreen, Jamie and I were sitting in front of the fire in our new flat above the fish and chip shop at Number 8, New Row off Upper St Martin's Lane in the centre of London. We were minding it for Nigel Green, another ex-RADA friend of Jamie's, who was at Stratford-upon-Avon with the Shakespearian Company for two years and had very kindly offered the flat to Doreen and me for two pound two shillings a week.

It had a nice bed-sitting room and a combined kitchen-bathroom. You could have a bath and chat to the person doing the cooking. Very cosy. The dunny was on the landing.

It was heaven after the first two weeks of our marriage. Our honeymoon was spent in a bed-sitter in Chalk Farm. That was my 'Gunga Din' period. The room had no water so I had to carry it in buckets from the bathroom in the basement.

'*Ssssh*! Listen!'

We could hear the creaking of the stairs . . . the light step of a female and the heavy tread of a man. They arrived at the landing on the next floor up. The door was opened and they moved to the centre of the room right above us.

'He's now paying the agreed sum of money.'

The bed squeaked.

'He's sitting on the edge of the bed taking his shoes off.'

Thump.

'One shoe.'

Thump.

'That's the other shoe.'

'Now he's getting his gear off.'

And pretty soon after that the bed started squeaking in earnest.

'Squeaky old bed,' said Jamie.

'Yeah. Doreen and I wondered if we should ask her to oil the springs. It's going to be very distracting when I'm learning lines.'

The room above us was occupied by a friendly prostitute more or less at the end of her career. She was no oil-painting and could only get the 'desperates'. Some nights there was no business at all . . . she would just come home and

drink. No squeaks. Just the odd clink of a glass. A lonely lady getting drunk.

The rooms above her were occupied by three sisters 'straight out of Dickens' as Doreen put it.

All in all, an interesting place for a student actor and his bride to live.

eleven

DON'T WORRY OLD MAN, HUMPHREY BOGART HAS A LISP

BEING AN EX-SERVICEMAN, I was about the oldest in the class, the youngest being Joan Collins, a sixteen year old who made even the most ordinary of sweaters look good. It was the time of the sweater girls; Ann Sheridan and Lana Turner were the Hollywood versions but I can tell you, a lot of the girls at RADA would have given them a run for their money.

I'd been well aware of this at the welcoming talk given by Sir Kenneth Barnes on our first day. The theatre seemed to be filled with 'sweater girls'. A bit of a worry, I'd only been married a couple of weeks.

The roll was called and my first class at RADA was about to begin ...

Voice production with the famous Clifford Turner.

'We will start with a little reading so that I

can get an idea of your voices. You all have your Shakespeares? The men will read "Henry V" and the ladies will read the "Nurse/Juliet" scene, *Romeo and Juliet*, Act 3 Scene 2—in alphabetical order. Carry on until I say "Next". Right, Vincent Ball.'

Bloody hell! That's the worst part of having a name like Ball . . . always at the top of the list.

The dreaded 'Chorus' speech. I hadn't done it since my audition for Whitehall.

'*Oh for a muse of fire, that would ascend the brightest heaven of invention,*

A kingdom for a stage . . . '

My mouth was full of tongue—it was everywhere where it shouldn't be, and my sibilant 'S' was starting to make an appearance. Why doesn't he say 'Next'?

Shit, here comes 'puissance'.

'*For the which supply, admit me chorus to this history,*

Who Prologue-like your humble patience pray,

Gently to hear, kindly to judge . . .'

'Next!'

Mr Turner had a look on his face that said, God! And I've got him for two years! The rest

of the class were staring at me, some had their mouths open.

'Yes, Vincent ... er—good,' said Mr Turner, writing something beside my name. 'Well, we ... er ... have a bit of ... ah ... work to do there, haven't we?'

'Yes, Mr Turner.'

'Next.'

As the men battled with Henry V in various accents and the girls with Juliet and the Nurse, I thought, what am I doing here? I've come to the *wrong* country. Where do they make westerns in Britain? They don't! And the chances of being 'discovered' in some remote Rep company after RADA must be pretty slim! Also, I'd be twenty-seven years old by the time I finished.

'Position two ... now, plié.'

I was in an old pair of Rugby shorts, hanging onto a rail being taught ballet. It was the second class on the first day. I can't see Buck Jones, Tom Mix or even John Wayne going through all this!

'Vincent, make the plié and the arm movement *flow* together ... more graceful ... and just a little inclination of the head.'

'Yes, Madame Sokalova.'

Maybe if I didn't get to Hollywood to be a cowboy, I might, if I was good enough, get parts in those swashbuckling films and those ones about the pioneer days in India and Australia. That'd be pretty close ... I'd have a horse and a six-gun. Maybe I'd get to play a bushranger ... Yeah!

'Vincent, can you turn your feet out further, like Mary in front of you. And concentrate!'

'Yes, Madame Sokalova.'

I have to be honest, 'Mary in front of me' was a bit of a worry. She was only *just* in front of me and all that movement in her small, tight shorts was very distracting. Well, anyway, what with her and the cowboys and my Rugby-muscled legs, it *was* difficult. Yeah, that's what I'll do. Work hard, get a bit of an English accent and maybe get some of those parts that Errol Flynn and Douglas Fairbanks Jnr played! Yeah, and ...

'That's better, Vincent! Right out, good boy!'

Boy, I thought ...

'Yes, Madame Sokalova.'

'Darling, how was your first day at the Royal Academy of Dramatic Art?' asked Doreen.

'Real good. I think I'm gunna like it.'

I had been sleeping pretty badly for the past few months and seemed to spend most nights staring at the ceiling, waiting for the metal churns to be delivered to the dairy next door at three am and Covent Garden to start at five am. Doreen didn't help by gently breathing at my side, getting her usual eight hours.

Whether it was the lack of sleep, the war, the excitement of starting at RADA, too many cigarettes and too much booze, I don't know, but I'd been getting pains around the solar plexus area for sometime now, so Doreen bundled me off to Charing Cross Hospital where, after various tests, they informed me that I had duodenal ulcers.

I was given pills to put me to sleep, pills to wake me up, pills to reduce acidity and enough pamphlets and instructions to choke a horse: no fried foods, no cigarettes, no alcohol, no stress but lots and lots of milk, etc, etc. What a mess.

Never mind about going to Hollywood, I'll be bloody lucky if I get through RADA.

As You Like It was our first full-length play. It was to be performed in a rehearsal room

without an audience as we were considered not up to the required standard to use the theatre. This was my second go at Shakespeare and I was one of six Orlandos. Ethel Carrington our teacher, a sweet, gentle lady, old fashioned in the nicest possible way, summed up my efforts with, 'Vincent, yours was a robust physical perform-ance, you handled the wrestling scene with Charles very well indeed. More light and shade vocally.'

I was finding, at twenty-five, the routine of classes hard to take and before long had devel-oped 'a sore ankle' which precluded me from ballet and dancing. I still managed to attend fencing and movement.

Movement was with Mr Dunstable, a neat little man who wore the smallest, tightest shorts possible and was obsessed, it seemed, with the pelvic movement of American sailors during the war. He was determined that we 'actor chappies' would achieve a similar movement and had a very 'friendly' habit of standing behind you with his hands on your hips and rotating your lower trunk, while breathing heavily on your neck.

Physical contact on the Rugby field was one thing. This was something else.

'Vincent, could I have a word with you?'

'Yes, Miss Brown.'

Miss Nancy Brown was the secretary of the Academy and was the one who really ran RADA.

'I understand that you haven't been attending movement classes?'

'That's right, Miss Brown.'

'Why is that?'

'Well, Miss Brown, I didn't want to cause Mr Dunstable any embarrassment in the classroom, but I had decided that if he put his hands on me once more and tried to rotate my lower trunk, I was going to have to have a quiet word with him. I thought it would be best for everyone if I stopped attending classes.'

A very flustered Miss Brown said, 'Oh yes ... well ... I ... er ... hope that you are utilising your time to good advantage and er ... yes.'

'Yes, Miss Brown. I do voice production exercises to correct my sibilant "S".'

'Oh good,' she said, quickly moving away.

My attitude was all wrong for the Royal Academy of Dramatic Art. Instead of trying to get the most from the course and the teachers,

who had so much to give, I was somehow managing to miss a lot of classes either by claiming to have to see the doctor or to have teeth extracted or filled, but in reality working for Ronnie Curtis at the Guild House Producers earning five pounds a day on documentaries for the Defence and Police forces.

Towards the end of the first term, Gee Martin rang me and asked if it was possible to get a day off to do a reading for a part in an Irish film being shot at Pinewood Studios called *Talk of a Million*, to be directed by John Paddy Carstairs.

'No worries,' I said.

It was about time I had another 'extraction'. At the rate I was going *on paper* I wouldn't have a tooth left in my head.

I read with two Irish actors from the Abbey Theatre, Dublin. Their Irish accent was perfect, of course. Mine was real stage bog Irish—it was terrible. The Irish actors had the good grace not to laugh out aloud when I started reading. They just paused, looked at each other, raised their eyebrows and carried on. All very embarrassing.

Three days later my agent told me that the film company wanted me to do a film test.

Another 'visit' to the dentist was out of the question, so I fronted up to Miss Brown and told her about the test and that if I got the part I would need ten weeks off from RADA.

Miss Brown, bless her, went to bat for me with Sir Kenneth, who gave me permission for the test and wished me luck.

I got the part and for the next ten weeks entered the world of feature films. The stars were Jack Warner and Barbara Mullen and I was to play one of their sons. The other supporting actors included Ronan O'Casey, Syd James, Noel Purcell and Alfie Bass.

It was ten weeks of beautiful locations in the Cotswolds, being wined and dined in *ye olde world* hotels, signing autographs for the locals, who were heard to mutter 'Vincent who?'.

Back to reality and RADA and one of six Romeos for our class's production of *Romeo and Juliet*, our first play in the theatre.

I was going pretty well, had got through the first couple of speeches of the 'Balcony' scene and was really starting to *feel* the part.

JULIET: What man art thou, that, thus bescreened in night so stumblest on my

counsel? *O-ooh* ...
(Doth my eyes deceive me or is the whole bloody balcony with a white-faced Juliet moving towards me? It was.)

ROMEO: (Me, leaping forward and holding the balcony in an upright position. What is it about *Romeo and Juliet* and me? We attract disaster.) By a name, I know not how to tell thee who I am ...

And that's how I played the famous 'Balcony' scene, propping up the balcony with one arm and at the same time trying to do justice to Shakespeare's poetic words to a terrified Juliet.

The ritual after each performance in the theatre was that the cast would gather in Sir Kenneth's office for notes.

'Vincent Ball, Tybalt,' said Sir Kenneth.

I must have gone real well, he couldn't remember which part I played.

'No, Sir Kenneth, Romeo.'

'Ah yes ... yes ... er ... a very er ... physical performance, a bit too casual I

thought, leaning against the balcony like that.'

'Thank you, Sir Kenneth.'

The following week I stood centre stage clutching the hand of Jacqueline Hill, the Nurse, in the longest 'dry' in the history of RADA, leaving out part of the important plot of *Romeo and Juliet* and having the embarrassment of the audience slowly chanting as though talking to a child,

> *And stay, good nurse, behind the abbey*
> *wall*
> *Within the hour my man shall be with*
> *thee*
> *And bring the cords made like a tackled*
> *stair,*
> *Which to the high top gallant of my joy*
> *Must be my convoy in the secret night.*

If only the night would swallow me up.

Our little flat at New Row above the fish and chip shop became a meeting place and watering hole for a large circle of budding actors—Stanley Baker, Bob Shaw, Donald Houston, Bill Sylvestor, Harold Jamieson, Frederick Treves, Nigel Green—and our kitchen floor the temporary abode for the odd homesick student.

New Row is off Upper St Martins Lane, the home of The Salisbury, the actors' pub, which was about fifty yards from our flat. Doreen and I would turn off the lights before closing time, hoping the darkness would deter our friends from paying us a visit. It never did. There'd be a loud banging on the door, followed by, 'Open up, we know you're in there.'

It was a good two years at RADA; a carefree time of living in the centre of London and paying our way with Doreen working at places like the Ideal Home and Selfridges, and me doing Lyons Cadby Hall during the holidays and the Post Office at Christmas. Mixed in with that were the classes and plays at RADA, struggling with the various dialects and parts, and having a quiet beer with Clifford Turner and Alexander Archdale.

Choral speaking with Frederick Ranilow was a bit of a worry. I'd been on *The Road to Samarkand* for months it seemed, with no end in sight. Never got to Samarkand; never got the hang of it. But I was congratulated on my 'tree in a storm' during a special movement class. It seems I was pretty good at the physical side of acting, like wrestling with Charles in *As You*

Like It, holding up the balcony in *Romeo and Juliet* and fencing. I suppose it was years of thinking 'cowboy'. They were men of few words, who let their guns do their talking.

I took Clifford Turner for a beer on my last day and mentioned that I still had an Australian accent, a bit of a lisp and a sibilant 'S'.

'Don't worry, old man,' said Clifford. 'Australians are very popular at the moment and Humphrey Bogart has a lisp.'

The next day, the lisp, sibilant 'S' and thick lazy tongue were the least of my problems. I couldn't bloody believe it, she had just given me the cue for my exit line, cutting out two and a half pages of my best part of the scene in *Royal Family*. Two years at the Royal Academy of Dramatic Art and my big chance to show the critics and agents what I can do in our graduation public show at the New Theatre and this happens.

I gave her the cue again, hoping she'd get back on the right track. Again she gave me my exit cue. She seemed frozen. I know the feeling only too well.

Stuff this, I thought. I'm not going off-stage until I've done my bit. So I proceeded to tear around the stage like a chicken with its head cut

off, running all my speeches together, determined to show them what I could do.

As we came off-stage, my leading lady said, 'I'm sorry. I'm so sorry.' And she meant it.

This after two years at the Royal Academy of Dramatic Art. I felt sick.

All the papers next day had reviews of our public show and most of the class got mentioned—'a deep and meaningful performance', 'the sweet cadences of her voice', 'shows promise', 'future star'—and there at last, my name. After two years my one and only mention: 'Vincent Ball looked splendid in jodphurs.'

It's no wonder my first job was in a bakelite factory at Mitcham.

Twelve

SEMI-RETIRED

I ACTUALLY FEEL LIKE I've been semi-retired since the day I left RADA in 1951. Looking back on it all, I don't suppose my career was much different from that of hundreds of other aspiring actors. Lots of ups and lots and lots of downs.

Well, you couldn't say my career had got off to an auspicious start, could you, with the job in the bakelite factory? They mistook my industry as keenness to get on and offered me a permanent position on the staff. I said no, thanked them, and left.

They didn't realise that the only reason I was working extra hard was because it helped the time to pass more quickly. Besides, that free pint of milk I was given each day to protect my lungs from the dust was a bit of a worry.

So, I moved from the bakelite dust to the sweet sickly smell at Paynes chocolate factory in

Croydon. I believe that every child should spend at least a day watching chocolate being made. Not only will it turn them off chocolate for life but will also save them a fortune in dentist bills and pimple cream.

Doreen and I, with the help of her parents, had acquired a small, semi-detached house in Carshalton, Surrey. That was after telling a few lies on the suggestion of the real estate agent whose reaction to being told that I was an actor, was: 'Oh no!'

'What's wrong with being an actor?' I asked.

'Everything,' he said. 'Actors, publicans and bookmakers are considered bad risks. You'll never get a mortgage. Why not say you're a *bookkeeper* and have a regular job. Can you get somebody to say they *employ* you?'

I rang Gee Martin and put the proposition to her. She agreed, and that's how Doreen and I became the proud possessors of a mortgage with the Halifax Building Society and that's why I was working in Paynes chocolate factory at Croydon and Doreen was working at the Festival of Britain. The mortgage had to be paid.

What was all that about 'the carefree life of

an actor'? Here I was just starting out, I already had a mortgage, I was working in a chocolate factory and I was twenty-eight years old. The way things were going I could end up being the oldest sheriff in the business.

Doreen had just told me she was pregnant. The year was 1952. It was one of the best years; one of the ups. I was going to be a father.

Then, out of the blue, I was offered the second male lead in two 'B' pictures being made back-to-back at Ealing Studios with a nice old Hollywood actor, Richard Arlen, as the lead. Films were made back-to-back because it was cheaper and as it was still the days of double features there was a need for 'B' pictures. Anyway, I was Arlen's doctor friend in the first film and his young lawyer friend in the second.

On the first day of shooting, Richard Arlen called the director aside and started going through the script crossing out most of his dialogue and leaving me with all the big speeches. He must be crazy, I thought.

Next day at the 'rushes' there on the screen was Richard Arlen in the foreground, in a mid close-up, playing with a piece of rope and every now and then uttering, 'Yeah,' 'No,' 'Huh, huh,'

while this disembodied voice, mine, came out of a pair of knees that wandered about in the background. Richard Arlen was not crazy, just very experienced.

Our lovely daughter Catherine Anne, was born on 8 December 1952 and brought with her a lot of joy, a new responsibility and cancelled out any disappointments I may have had so far in show business.

I don't know whether my skills as an actor were improving, but I can tell you that I had developed into a first-class labourer, painter and an expert cheese-and-pickle sandwich maker for Joe Lyons at Cadby Hall. As far as my stage career went, things were put into the right perspective when I had an offer to go to Stratford-upon-Avon as the rear end of a donkey in their Christmas pantomime, with the guarantee of then staying for the Shakespearian season. Maybe I should have taken it because it was the only offer I ever had from Stratford.

Doreen's parents retired and arrived from Sarawak in 1953. They stayed with us for a short time before buying a cottage in Kenley, Surrey. During their stay, I was understudying

Michael Denison and Ronald Lewis in a play called *The Bad Samaritan*. Also in the cast was Virginia McKenna, a lovely, friendly, talented actress whom I called 'My English Rose'. We toured for nine weeks and finished up at the Criterion, Piccadilly Circus, where after a few weeks I asked for my release because I'd been offered a part in another 'B' picture with a Hollywood actor, William Lundigan. The film, *Dangerous Voyage*, was to be shot in Deauville, France.

It was a lousy script but I was quickly learning that I couldn't afford to turn down work no matter how bad it was. My life was ruled by economics.

Doreen and I were finding that the suburbia of Carshalton was the wrong place for us. We had splendid neighbours but we were like fish out of water, so we sold up and moved in with an actor friend, Sydney Bromley, at Woldingham. Most people I know make a profit when they buy and sell a house. But not us. We bought our little semi-detached for 2750 pounds, decorated it, inside and out, built a garage and installed a hot water system and then sold it for 2500 pounds!

I was beginning to think I made other actors

look good, which was a bit of a worry. I'm not sure whether it was because I was so bad that it made them look good or I was so good that it put them on their mettle and they looked even better. But whatever it was, it wasn't working for me.

Roger Moore and I did a couple of things together and he ended up getting a 20th Century Fox film contract. Stephen Boyd and I did a full-length BBC television play, with me playing the lead and he was immediately snapped up by the film studios. What was I doing?

I was loading bales of hay onto a bloody big wagon in the Woldingham valley, being employed by the local convent to help with the harvest. It was the first and only time I worked for the Pope. I just hoped that whoever was keeping score 'up there in the big book' would tell the patron saint of show business that I was giving a 100 per cent down here and if Roger Moore and Stephen Boyd can go to Hollywood and play cowboys, what about an Irish-Australian Catholic actor who was helping the nuns bring in the harvest?

The bill at the hotel in Norfolk was quite substantial.

I was up there doing a children's film for the Mary Field Film Foundation and Doreen and Cathy had joined me for a couple of weeks. It was a chance for them to have an inexpensive holiday ... or so I thought.

Cathy, the clever little angel, managed to flood our bedroom. She put the plug in the hand-basin and turned on both taps so that the water eventually dripped through the dining-room ceiling and larder during the evening meal.

This bit of bad luck was balanced by a call from my agent to say that Jack Lee and Joe Janni wanted to see me at Heathrow Airport. They were about to make *A Town Like Alice* with Peter Finch and Virginia McKenna. Jack Lee was on his way to Malaya to shoot background locations.

It was the time when most Australian actors were supposed to be tall, lean, rolled their own and looked like Chips Rafferty. I don't look like Chips Rafferty.

The interview lasted all of three minutes. Jack Lee shooks hands with all of us and left. Mrs Janni turned to her husband and said, 'Joe, will you put Vincent out of his misery and tell him he's got the part.'

'As the producer, *I'm* supposed to tell him that. I like telling people good news,' Joe said to me. 'You've got the part of Ben. Congratulations.'

A few weeks later Doreen, Cathy and I moved into 25 Harben Road, Swiss Cottage. Our next-door neighbours were John and Penelope Mortimer. John Mortimer was a practicing Queen's Counsellor and was just embarking on a writing career with a one-act play called *Dock Brief*.

Going near the wire surrounding the POW camp was out of bounds, punishable with a beating from the Japanese guards with their split-bamboo canes. That's what it said in the script of *A Town Like Alice*.

Finchie was to rush to the wire because he'd spotted Ginny and the other ladies on their forced march to nowhere, and I was to rush after him and drag him back before the guards spotted him. Well it wasn't going too well.

'You are nasty, horrible, vicious, cruel, terrible Japanese guards and you hate these Australian prisoners. I want you to be rough with them. Drag them and I mean *drag* them back

from the wire. They will struggle but you must overpower them ... you understand? ... *Overpower* them. Okay, let's do it again.'

Jack Lee, our director, was going slightly berserk trying to get the Japanese guards, who were actually Chinese waiters from all the Chinese restaurants in Soho, to behave as Japanese guards really behaved.

It was about take four and Finchie and I were exhausted. We were trying to make the scene look authentic but we had no one to fight except a bunch of lovely, friendly, giggling Chinese waiters. They were so gentle and apologetic that we weren't getting anywhere and in between takes they handed out cards of their restaurants with the offer of a free meal.

Finally they did get into the spirit of the thing and after the final take Finchie and I surveyed the damage. We were covered from head to foot with little red marks. Every time they grabbed us, they pinched us. It was their idea of being vicious. Perhaps it was an old form of Chinese torture!

A Town Like Alice was one of the highs of my career. Peter Finch was great to work with, helpful, one of the boys. He became a mate and,

of course, there was 'My English Rose' Virginia McKenna.

On the set next to ours Kenneth More was filming *Reach for the Sky* and it seems they had a problem with the actor playing Muriel Pavlow's cousin. It was a small scene in a cafe and the producer asked Jack if he could borrow me for an hour. Jack agreed and within a very short time I was having tea and cucumber sandwiches with Muriel Pavlow, speaking my six lines with my back to the camera.

I wouldn't be *discovered* in *Reach for the Sky*.

On the final day of *Alice* we were all in the bar at Pinewood having a few drinks when Jack Lee took me aside.

'You did a good job. I suppose you think it was your personality or whatever that got you the part.'

'I don't know,' I said. 'Why did I get the part?'

'Well, when Ginny rang us saying she liked the script, she also mentioned that Vincent Ball would be right for the part of Ben. I said, who is Vincent Ball? Write the name down so you won't forget it, she said. I wrote the name down.

That's how you got the part. Thank Ginny.'

All through my career I found that a lot of the time, it's the people you know who get you the part.

Theo Cowan, publicity director for J. Arthur Rank Films, was showing a group of dignitaries around Pinewood Studios and as he stepped into the main building he was confronted by two of J. Arthur Rank's top actors, Peter Finch and Pat McGoohan, pissed out of their minds, attempting with their bare hands to tear the heads off the two stone lions guarding the building. Theo tried to distract the goggle-eyed tourists as Finchie lost his battle with the lion and tumbled down the cement steps, leaving a trail of blood from his nose. I witnessed all this and Theo's frantic signalling of 'Get him outa here'. I helped Finchie to his feet and half carried him to the carpark and dumped him in the back of my car, where he gave a quick rendition of 'Click Go the Shears' and slept like a baby all the way back to London where I delivered this rather battered actor to 'Ma', his mother.

'Hello Noddy, how are you today?'

I bent over the little wooden puppet, which

nodded and jigged up and down near my right
ear, supposedly whispering to me.

'You're very excited because you've invited
Mr Plod and Big Ears to tea ... and you've
... what? Made them a cake ... a chocolate
cake.'

What the bloody hell was I doing talking to
a wooden puppet in a log cabin on a show called
'Junior Television', when, if things had gone the
way I had hoped, I would have been riding the
range in a Hollywood western?

Well, quite simply, I was offered the job by
a mate of mine, John Terry, and I accepted.

'Junior Television' had an hour and a half
time slot and I had to fill in the time not taken
up by the commercials and three films, *Noddy*,
Roy Rogers and *Robin Hood*. That left me with
between ten and fifteen minutes which, when
you don't sing or play a musical instrument, is a
long time and a lot of wordies.

A Town Like Alice was released in early
1956 and was a great success. J. Arthur Rank
offered me a film contract, starting with a salary
of thirty pounds a week. Lew Grade of ATV
offered me 100 pounds a week, to compere
'Junior Television' and do the odd, one-off

interviews for the London Palladium promotions. I said yes to the 100 pounds, on condition they contracted Harold Jamieson as my script writer. ATV agreed.

'Junior Television' gave me celebrity status. One newspaper referred to me as 'the housewife's heart-throb'. I imagine it was because I kept their kids quiet and off the streets.

I was doing six shows a week and getting about 500 letters a week. Lew Grade gave me a secretary, the lovely Brenda Ennis, to cope with it all. Dear, patient Brenda.

Our son Christian David was born at one am on 20 September 1956 at the Nursing Home, Avenue Road, St Johns Wood, London. Unfortunately I wasn't around for the birth. I was on my way to interview Liberace and his brother George aboard the *Queen Mary*, which was docking at Southhampton that same morning. It was to be advance publicity for his Palladium show.

Liberace had been dealing with reporters and interviewers for most of his life, especially ones who try to be clever. So when I asked him the smart-arsed question, 'If he would ever

marry?', he smiled and with a twinkle in his eyes said, 'Yes ... Yes, when the right lady comes along.'

I arrived as a sceptic and left as a fan.

The arrival of Christian started a series of live-in au-pairs, who kept him shining like a new button, a happy, contented, gurgling bonny boy. A real live doll for his sister Cathy to play with.

I was now thirty-four years old and so far Hollywood seemed to be getting along quite well without me. My dream was slowly receding along with my hairline.

Joe Janni and Jack Lee were preparing to make the Australian Classic *Robbery Under Arms* and had offered me the small part of George Storefield. I accepted it because it meant a trip to Australia.

A week later they informed me that the part would now be shot in England. They were building a replica of a small bush town behind Pinewood Studios. I turned it down. Maybe I was getting a big head. What was that saying? 'There's no such thing as a small part, only small actors.'

Anyway, after a particularly boozy lunch at Pinewood with Finchie, Joe and Jack, I agreed

to play the part, as Joe put it, 'For old times sake. You never know in our business, anything can happen.'

I thought he gave me what I can only describe as 'a knowing look'.

The film unit had only been in Australia three weeks when Joe rang me from Adelaide asking if it was possible to get time off from 'Junior Television' and come out to Australia. ATV agreed, Gerry Campion stood in for me, and I took off for Australia.

'Junior Television' was on air at the time when the Australian Government was trying to entice English immigrants on the 'ten pound' scheme to settle in Australia. As I spent most Sundays on television talking about and showing the nicest aspects of my country, that is, the golden beaches, the rainforests, the Snowy Mountains, Sydney Harbour and any other promotional film showing Australia at its best, the government couldn't do enough for me when it was announced that I was off to Australia to do a film.

The Australian Government said that I had, through 'Junior Television', given their immigration programme about 100,000 pounds worth of

free publicity and so I was offered a chauffeur-driven limousine for twenty-four hours a day while in Sydney.

By the time I had reached Singapore the producers had re-scheduled the scenes with George, so that they would be shot in England, behind Pinewood Studios. Joe Janni didn't have the heart to send me back. Dear Joe.

To earn my keep in Australia they did eventually give me one momentous line, '*What are they doing about the government contracts?*'

And I was in the country for ten weeks on full pay.

While we were in Adelaide and up in Wilpena Pound, Ford Motors lent me a big Galaxie to drive around in. My old mate Bruce Burton was one of the Ford directors. I don't think Bruce would mind now, but Finchie and I used the Galaxie to go kangaroo shooting at night.

The rest of the time was spent being chauffeur driven around Sydney. Mum and Dad were most impressed, seeing this big black government limousine parked outside the house at Waitara.

After I returned to England, the question

was raised in Canberra about the misuse of government cars. Apparently it would have been cheaper to buy me a car: the chauffeurs were on double time after five pm.

'Ah Vincent, Victor. Come up to my dressing room and have a chat.'

It was more like a command than a request.

'Yes, Sir Donald.' Sir Donald, being, Sir Donald Wolfit, one of the truly 'big' actors of the theatre.

It was obvious we all needed money, because we were at Twickenham Studios doing a little horror flick called *Blood of the Vampire*. Sir Donald was the vampire, Victor Maddern his deformed assistant Igor, Barbara Shelley the heroine and I was Pierre, the hero.

It was almost a daily ritual: Sir Donald would recline on his couch talking mainly of the Shakespearian plays and other classics that he had done on Broadway and in the West End. We were fascinated by this grand old actor, never interrupting, an incongruous pair quietly sitting there, Victor with his hump and an eye in the middle of his left cheek, me with a little Van Dyke beard and a frilly shirt with puffed sleeves.

Then it would be back to the reality of earning our bread and butter in the papier-mâché castle on the studio floor below, which stank to high heaven as the entrails of cows in jars of water slowly went off under the hot studio lights. The jars and their contents were dressing for the vampire's laboratory. It was a low budget film, apparently they couldn't afford formalin!

'Hello Noddy, what are you doing today?'

'Noddy, I said, what are you doing today?'

Why doesn't the little bugger answer me, instead of jumping up and down like that?

'Noddy . . . what . . . are . . . you . . .'

Good God, I must be going bonkers. I'm waiting for a wooden puppet to answer me! I quickly leaned forward and said, 'Sorry Noddy, I was daydreaming. You're what?'

'You're going off to the dark wood to see Golliwog.'

Daydreaming? I was going off my rocker. I'd been talking to Noddy for four years now and was trapped by the regular money and the perks that came with it. I was becoming known as a TV personality.

I had to make the break, but how? I was then aged thirty-five, supporting a wife, two children, an au-pair, a car and a lifestyle that I was used to.

My prayers were answered two days later in the form of a telephone call from Monty Berman, offering me a role in his new film *Sea of Sand* that was being shot in North Africa. I accepted and gave in my notice to ATV.

On my last programme I took my viewers on that great ride with 'The Man from Snowy River' just as I had done on my first show four years previously. In those years, I had told them about my upbringing in the bush, the pioneering days, the folklore heroes, the explorers, boundary riders, blacktrackers, bushrangers, the flying doctors, drovers, brumbies and, with the help of film and poets such as Banjo Paterson, Henry Lawson and Will Ogilvy, illustrated to them the comradeship, the courage, the humour and pioneering spirit of the early settlers.

Maybe they would remember just a bit of it. And for your benefit my dear grandchildren, perhaps a particular Australian verandah that I had told them about on Sunday 22 October 1957:

Junior Television

You know most of the stories I tell you are about pioneers, whose courage, determination and sacrifice have made them famous and they now form part of our Australian history. But I think there were thousands and thousands of unsung pioneers who quietly went about the business of living and raising a family. And where would any new country be without those precious families?

I've always regarded my family in this way. We lived in places like Wee Waa and Moree, up near the Queensland border. Dad was a senior linesman, which meant that he would disappear for two or three months at a time putting up telegraph poles out in the bush and, I suppose, in his own small way help build up the communication system of Australia. My mum, bless her, was quite a pioneer in her own way too, raising seven healthy kids in the Australian bush was no mean feat.

The memories of all those rabbits we ate . . . memories.

I don't suppose many of you younger viewers are really old enough to have stored up important memories. It's only when the lines begin to appear

and the old double chin starts moving in, that the mind looks back over its shoulder at the past. The strange and I think pleasant part about memory is that the mind is inclined to remember only the happy associations, it pushes the unpleasant memories conveniently into the background. Perhaps you've heard your dad say, 'Oh, things were much better in my day'. Well, perhaps they were and then again perhaps they weren't. I'm sure you will all store up memories that will live with you for the rest of your lives ... a favourite corner in the house you used to live in, the armchair near the window with the trees outside, the toolshed at the bottom of the garden; places associated with happy events and times.

One place that I find myself constantly remembering is the old wooden house in Wee Waa, with a galvanised roof, and in front of that house was a verandah. The verandah plays a very important part in the social life of Australia. It's a place where the family and friends congregate in the evenings and at weekends; where you discuss the weather, the crops, the town gossip and where you put the world to rights. It's also the place where my father performed an amazing athletic feat: he leapt two feet in the air from a

sitting position. He was helped in this remarkable gymnastic display by the fact that a poisonous snake had slid down the vine-covered verandah post and bitten him on the right knee. As he jumped, with my baby sister Noni in his arms, he yelled, 'Snake!' Then bedlam broke loose. Seven children, two dogs, one cat, two parents and one lonely little snake turned that verandah into a madhouse. The family took off inside and the snake, deciding that this was no place for him, took off into the garden. We packed Dad off to hospital and he was back as right as rain in a week. Perhaps this doesn't seem to you to be a pleasant memory, but when I think back on it, all I can remember is the comedy and chaos that followed that one dramatic incident. It's still good for a laugh when the family get together. And the verandah, to me, is still a pleasant memory because it was:

> *Here that we spun out stories of saddle and stirrup*
> *To drift through the vine and be lost in the stars,*
> *While countless cicadas with challenging chirrup*

Would deafen the dark in the bunch of
    belars.
And far down that road we so often
    passed over
We'd glimpse the red rose of a campfire
    that tells
The long day is done for some teamster
    or drover,
And hear in the ridges the clash of his
    bells.

But time will not linger. What use of our
    hoarding
Those fanciful treasures of sound and of
    sight,
For other men's rowels now ring on that
    boarding
And other men bow to those spells of the
    night.
Goodbye and farewell to that distant
    verandah,
Its moonlight and magic and whispering
    trees,
And all that they mean to an exiled
    wanderer,
Who send them his greeting from over the
    seas.

And then there was the comradeship. The comradeship of other people is one of the best things to have in life, and one of the most difficult to recapture because circumstances and people change. They go their different ways, assume new responsibilities, and that sincere promise of I'll drop you a line is kept up, maybe for a couple of years and then finally dwindles until all contact is lost. And if and when you meet again, try as you may, you can't quite recapture the same spirit of comradeship that bound you together in the earlier years. Henry Lawson sums it up pretty well in his poem 'Since Then':

> *I met Jack Ellis in town today . . .*
> *Jack Ellis . . . my old mate, Jack.*
> *Ten years ago, from the Castlereagh,*
> *We carried our swags together, away*
> *To the Never-Again, Out Back.*
>
> *But times have altered since those old days,*
> *And the times have changed the men.*
> *Jack Ellis and I have tramped long ways*
> *On different tracks since then.*
> *His hat was battered, his coat was green,*

The toes of his boots were through,
But the pride was his! It was I felt mean ...
I wished that my collar was not so clean,
Nor the clothes I wore so new.

He saw me first, and he knew 'twas I ...
The holiday swell he met.
And he made as though he would pass me by,
For he thought that I might forget.

He ought to have known me better than that,
By the tracks we tramped far out ...
The sweltering scrub and the blazing flat,
When the heat came down through each old
    felt hat
In the hell-born western drought.

He took my hand in a distant way
(I thought how we parted last)
And we seemed like men who have nought to
    say
And who meet ... 'Good-day,' and who part
    'Good-day,'
Who never have shared the past.

I asked him in for a drink with me ...
Jack Ellis ... my old mate, Jack ...
But his manner no longer was careless and free,

He followed, but not with the grin that he
Wore always in the days Out Back.
I tried to live in the past once more ...
Or the present and past combine,
But the days between I could not ignore ...
I couldn't but notice the clothes he wore,
And he couldn't but notice mine.

He placed his glass on the polished bar,
And he wouldn't fill up again;
For he is prouder than most men are ...
Jack Ellis and I have tramped too far
On different tracks since then.

He said that he had a mate to meet,
And 'I'll see you again,' said he,
Then he hurried away through the crowded
    street,
And the rattle of buses and scrape of feet
Seemed suddenly loud to me.

Sea of Sand was without doubt the best film location I'd ever been on. The all-male cast consisted of Richard Attenborough, John Gregson, Michael Craig, Ray McAnally, Barry Foster, Percy Herbert, Andrew Faulds, George Murcell and myself.

The charter flight to Tripoli, Libya, set the tone for the whole location. We played poker all the way.

The filming was pretty rugged and the temperature always around 100 plus, but nobody seemed to mind very much. There was always that refreshing shower after the hair-raising drive back from the desert then the night of poker.

Michael Craig and I hit it off right from the start, helped along every evening with a pre-dinner drink of a bottle of Scotch costing ten and three from the Army NAAFI.

'Your balcony or mine,' one of us would ask, and then we'd put the world to rights as the sky darkened and the lights appeared around Tripoli Harbour, finally dropping the empty bottle in the wastepaper basket on our way down to dinner.

'What are you doing after this, Snow?' Dickie asked.

'Nothing as far as I know.'

'I'm doing a POW film *Danger Within*, and there's a part of an Aussie adjutant which I think you'd be right for. I'll mention it to the producer, if it's alright with you?'

'Ah . . . yes . . . Thanks Dickie.'

My next film was *Danger Within*. Thanks to Richard Attenborough, who 'mentioned' me to the Producer. You see. People you know!

It was directed by Don Chaffey and the cast included Richard Attenborough, Richard Todd, Bernard Lee, Michael Wilding, Denis Price, Donald Houston and a very young Michael Caine.

It was a happy film, notable for its poker schools, frantic drives back to London and my meeting up with Don Chaffey. These were the days before random breath testing.

Always short of money, I began working for the Danzigers, a film company producing 'B' pictures at the rate of about one every ten days.

It was like a factory. I played the lead in about five of them, having the unique experience of being paid in cash at the end of each day.

It was pretty apparent by now that I wasn't going to be 'discovered' and whisked off to Hollywood. I had to face the fact that I was just a 'jobbing' actor, playing some leads in 'B' pictures and smallish supporting roles in first features. I'd had opportunities to be discovered but nothing had happened and I was getting a bit long in the tooth to be an 'up and coming young actor'.

'We're in the shit,' I said. 'All of us.'

Bill Kerr, Ed Deveraux, John Meillon, Ralph Petersen and myself were sitting in a pub in Shaftesbury Avenue having just attended an Equity meeting and somehow the conversation got around to income tax. That's when I summed up the situation. At the time I was paying 25 per cent of my earnings to the tax people.

'We should form a club and call it the "WITS",' I said. 'WITS: we're ... in ... the ... shit. Get it?'

A few pints later the club was formed. Ralph was to be our president and would wear the badge of office: a terrible tie that had a kangaroo outlined in sequins on it and owned by John Meillon.

The purpose of the club was to do 'good works' within the profession. At the time it didn't sound too bad at all. Over the years we would meet monthly at Ken J. Warren's club The Kangaroo Paddock, just off Sloane Square, the minutes would be read and words like: order, out of order, bullshit and another red, were often used when discussing the 'business of the day'.

Leo McKern, Madge Ryan and Maggie Fitz-gibbon were our honorary members. I don't think we ever did any 'good works', but the meetings were great.

'Vincent, old man, it's Johnny Mills here. How are you? I wonder if you would do me a favour?'

'Ah, yes Johnny, if I can. What is it?'

This call was quite a surprise, we hadn't seen each other for a few years, since working together on *The Baby and the Battleship*.

'I'm going out to Australia to play Barney in *The Summer of the Seventeenth Doll*. They want to test my daughter Juliet for the part of Bubba. Would you help her with the Aussie accent?'

I agreed, and Juliet and I worked together for a couple of mornings. She was offered the part but Binkie Beaumont, the big West End pro-ducer, refused to release her from *Five Finger Exercise*, the play she was in at the Comedy Theatre. So much for all that.

About two weeks later, I had another call from Johnny, would I help *him* with the Aussie accent? We worked all morning, had lunch with two bottles of red, and that was it. All accents,

English and Australian, were distinctly slurred. We called it a day.

'Ring your agent,' Doreen said, when I arrived home. I did.

'I'll read you a cable I've just received from Hollywood,' said my agent. ' "Availability ... Vincent Ball ... The Summer of the Seventeenth Doll ... Australia ... December".'

'Well, what are you going to do?' asked Doreen.

For the past few months we had been collecting the numerous documents necessary for immigration to America. Doreen wasn't very happy about it but if I was that desperate to realise my dream, she'd go along with it. The US Embassy had informed us that the waiting period would be six weeks. It was 1959. Thirty-six is practically middle aged.

The lure of a nice part in an Aussie film being made for a Hollywood company and the chance to see Mum, Dad, my brothers and sisters again was too much. The *Doll* it would be.

The round ball came towards me on the green grass of the Arsenal football ground. I took a big

kick at it and fell arse over tit, feeling a sharp pain shooting up from my left ankle. I hobbled off to the dressing room, where the Arsenal masseur looked at it and said I'd sprained my ankle.

The reason I was at the Arsenal stadium trying to kick a round soccer ball was because I had agreed to be a member of a 'film eleven' to play the 'show biz' team in a charity match. This particular day was for familiarisation with the round ball and the rules of the game.

That night, my ankle came up like a balloon and was really throbbing. So much so, that I took myself off to Hampstead Hospital where they X-rayed my leg and informed me that I had a two inch spiral break in my fibula and my leg would need to be in plaster for about six to eight weeks.

'But I'm off to Australia to do a film in four weeks.'

'Sorry, but you won't be able to go. It needs to be put in plaster now.'

'I'll have it done tomorrow,' I said. 'Can I borrow the X-rays?'

I'd told my mum and dad that I was coming to Australia and there was no way that I was going to disappoint them and myself. But how do you do a film with a broken leg?

George Murcell, an actor mate, came up with a suggestion. 'Before you do anything rash, go and see this orthopaedic surgeon I know. He's the best in London and an old Rugby man.'

'You must walk *without limping* and for God's sake, don't turn over on your ankle, otherwise the bone may come through the skin. I'll send you a physiotherapist daily. Your main bone will act as a splint. Remember, *don't limp*,' said the best orthopaedic surgeon in town.

I walked without a limp and the physio came every day.

The big hurdle would be the film insurance doctor who I had to visit before I left for Australia. I delayed seeing him for as long as possible, until the studio insisted that I make an appointment and *keep it*.

'Anything wrong with you that I should know about?' the doctor asked.

'No,' I replied, as casually as possible.

'I heard you'd hurt your ankle at soccer training?'

Oh shit, I thought, how did he know about that?

'Oh yes,' I said. 'I ricked my ankle a couple of weeks ago, but it's alright now. Nothing to

worry about,' jigging up and down on my toes.

'Well, I better have a look at it, just to make sure.'

I had on a pair of long Air Force socks rolled down about my ankles to cover any swelling.

I presented my foot, which he turned in a circular motion one way, then the other.

'Any pain?'

'No nothing,' I said, giving him that look that I'd seen Buck Jones, Tim McCoy and Tom Mix give when facing death. That steady, unwavering 'I'll die like a man' look. But I thought, if he turns my foot once more I'll scream the place down. He didn't.

'Cut,' said the director, Les Norman.

It was my first scene in Australia and I had to walk rather quickly across a road followed by Johnny Mills.

'Have you got a limp or something? You seem to be swinging your left leg out in a curve, sort of, favouring it a bit.'

'No Les, I've always walked like that.'

'Have you? Well, I've never noticed that before. Strange. Okay. Let's do it again.'

The *Doll* was another happy film, with Ernest Borgnine, Johnny Mills, Angela Lansbury, Anne Baxter, Ethel Gabriel, Jannette Craig, and enhanced by the visiting English cricket team and their most ardent supporter, Trevor Howard.

One memorable evening, the Test team and cast were all chatting and sipping champagne at a party Johnny Mills had given at his Point Piper residence. The only odd thing about this was that we were all standing in the swimming pool with the water lapping our chins and most of us fully clothed. It was Freddie Truman's idea.

The film company had installed me in a flat in Macleay Street, Kings Cross, with a per diem allowance and petrol vouchers for the 'courtesy car' organised by my old mate Bruce Burton of Ford Motors. It wasn't a bad life . . . for a while, but things were starting to get a little out of hand. Ernie Borgnine was in the habit of popping in with a bottle and after a few drinks would ring 'his woman', Katy Jurado in Hollywood, on my phone. Not that I minded, the film company was picking up the tab anyway. It was the booze that was the problem.

After two weeks of 'Life at the Cross', I rang big brother Brian and pleaded, 'Please can I come and stay with you for the rest of the filming?'

When I knocked on the door of his home in Eastwood I achieved a fleeting moment of immortality. The door was opened, with great difficulty, by my six-year-old nephew, Geoffrey, who had never seen me before. He looked up and said, 'Hello.'

'Hello. Would you tell your mum and dad that Vincent Ball is at the door.'

He stared at me in wonderment, his eyes wide with disbelief, backed away, turned and ran down the hallway calling out in a hushed, excited voice, 'Mum, Mum, Vincent de Paul is at the door ... it's Vincent de Paul, Mum, he's at the door ... Vincent de Paul ... Mum ... Vincent de Paul ...'

As I said, my fleeting moment of immortality.

Seeing all the family was a huge bonus. I promised Mum and Dad that I would bring their grandchildren out to see them as soon as possible.

The first champagne cork popped as the *Constellation* levelled out after take-off on our way back to the UK. I was travelling with the Mills family: Johnny, Mary, Hayley and Jonathan.

Ava Gardner, who was in Australia filming *On the Beach*, was being courted at the time by Walter Chiari, an Italian actor. He was on the same flight and appeared to be trying to drink the plane dry.

'I am very unhappy, very unhappy. May I join you?' he asked.

In that morning's press Ava Gardner had referred to their romance as being, 'As cold as a plate of yesterday's spaghetti'.

By the time we arrived at Singapore, I had agreed to pose as Johnny's publicist and stay with them while they were the guests of the Chinese millionaire filmmakers Run Run Shaw and Run Me Shaw.

A luxury bungalow by the water, turbanned servants, an air-conditioned Rolls Royce, Chinese meals consisting of thirty courses at our host's home. Being looked after by a beautiful Chinese film starlet from Hong Kong, who sat beside me at mealtimes picking out all the delicacies from the dishes and putting them on my

plate. Then a stroll through the softly lit gardens to the private cinema for liqueurs, cigars and a Brigette Bardot film. I tell you, my grandchildren, life as an actor can sometimes be hell.

The other side of the coin was hearing a cry from a partly constructed building and then looking up to see a workman falling through the bamboo scaffolding from about eight storeys above onto the cement pavement.

Life must have been cheap in Singapore, because nobody seemed concerned about the poor guy who fell. Everyone was standing around in groups, laughing and showing how the workman missed that ledge; bounced off that plank; hit this; missed that, etc. I can still see him falling, as in action replay, all in slow motion.

Dad never got to see his English grandchildren. He died three months after I returned to England. The year was 1960.

thirteen

THE HALCYON YEARS

WHILE MAKING *Danger Within*, Doreen and I had formed a strong friendship with Don and Edna Chaffey, who had on several occasions invited us to stay at their holiday cottage in Dymchurch on the Kentish coast. It was during these visits that we grew to love the Kent countryside.

Since Doreen's father's death, her mother had been living in a bed-sitter in Swiss Cottage, but having most of her meals with us. It wasn't a happy arrangement. The only solution, we decided, was to find a house big enough for all of us. London was too expensive so the Kentish countryside seemed to be the answer.

We spent most weekends there, looking at houses large and small, and becoming more attached to the countryside, with its oast houses, hop fields and orchards. Mentally we had left London.

The Old Rectory, Stowting, had been empty for two years. It was on two and a half acres, had a tithe barn, twenty-two rooms, beetles, damp rot and offered a challenge. For twelve months, winter and summer we picnicked on its lawns, stole the fruit, picked the flowers and dreamed.

'Before we make a bid, let's look at another county,' I suggested.

With my agent Gee Martin, Doreen and I spent three days in Sussex and all we thought about was the Old Rectory. Nothing compared with its acres of green lawns, roses, evergreens and rising above it all, the most beautiful copper beech tree you've ever seen.

'A gentleman's residence,' the surveyor from Canterbury said. It was the way he said it. I got the feeling that he didn't regard us as the *right people* for the Old Rectory and that got up my nose a bit. I looked at Doreen and she gave me the smallest of nods. At that moment we made up our minds to have this 'gentleman's residence'.

We bought the Old Rectory with the help of Dorcen's mum and our old friend, the Halifax Building Society, for 4000 pounds and moved in

on 9 December 1960. It was the best thing we ever did.

We tackled that place with all the enthusiasm of a couple of teenagers and my advice to any cash-poor male contemplating buying a very large house of about twenty-two rooms, which had been empty for two and half years, is to make sure his wife or girlfriend can sew!

Doreen made every curtain, chair-cover, bed-cover and most of her clothes. We turned the Rectory into a place that made our hearts beat a little faster as we caught sight of the big copper beech on the way home from Ashford, Canterbury or Folkestone.

These were the halcyon years.

'Once Aboard the Lugger', a children's serial with John Hurt and Lyn James, and a newspaper serial 'Deadline Midnight' for ATV kept the wolf from the door well into 1961. The selling of the tithe barn to Harold Jamieson helped solve the central heating problem.

A police car had been following me for some time now on the A20. It was about three am and I was on my way home from the 'wrap' party of 'Deadline Midnight'. I'd had a few and the

window was wound down to clear the air of any smell of alcohol that may have been about. Finally, the police car overtook me and flagged me down. Oh shit, I thought, here we go. I watched the constable amble towards me.

'Good morning, sir.'

'Good morning, constable.'

'Where are you going, sir?'

'Home ... Stowting.'

'Where have you come from, sir?'

'ATV Studios, Elstree. Why have you stopped me?'

'You looked suspicious. Driving without a coat with the window down on a very cold morning.'

'I have the heater on and ...'

'Aren't you?' he interrupted, peering at me closely. 'You look like ... er ... I've seen you before ... er ... you're er ...'

Same old story, knows the face, not the name.

'My name's Vincent Ball. I'm an actor.'

'Ah yes, of course. You used to do Noddy. Would you mind signing this for my little girl. She loved Noddy. She always called you Noddy's Dad.'

I signed a page in his police book.

'Thank you, sir. Have a safe drive home, sir,' giving me a funny old look.

As I watched him scream off into the darkness, I thought, he might have mentioned a few other things I'd done.

Noddy's Dad!

When I pulled into the drive, I noticed that the lights were still on in our bedroom. Bless her, Doreen was waiting up for me.

She was sitting up in bed reading an Agatha Christie, looking nice and cosy.

'You shouldn't have waited up. It's very late.'

'I thought you might like to know that I'm pregnant,' Doreen said. 'Surprised?'

'Very. You?'

'Very.'

Now Jonathan, there's no need to get uptight. You were *wanted*, we *planned* for you. You just arrived a little early that's all. Okay?

Michael Craig, Donald Houston and their families were spending Christmas 1961 with us. They all arrived on 20 December, 'to give them time to get the Christmas spirit,' they said.

By the look of the cases coming out of their cars, they brought most of the Christmas 'spirit' with them. These were good times.

Don Chaffey and his family also joined us. The weather did the right thing and gave us snow, the turkey was beautifully cooked by Michael, Donald and myself, and Doreen was six months pregnant. All the ingredients for a splendid Christmas. And it was, as Michael said, 'The best I've ever had.'

Jonathan Vincent was born at the Hythe Nursing Home on 10 April 1962. Another bonny boy.

I was in the middle of mowing the side lawn, when Doreen called out, 'Carl Foreman's on the phone. He wants to talk to you.'

As I quickly turned off the mower and headed towards the house, I thought, Carl Foreman, the famous producer-director wants to talk to me? This might be it—my big chance—at last, Hollywood here I come. I nervously picked up the phone.

'Hello, it's Vincent Ball.'

'Carl Foreman here. I saw your play on TV last night.' I waited for the compliment, but

instead, 'I wondered if you would do me a favour, Vincent?'

Now when a producer asks any jobbing actor to do them a favour, it usually means—they've run out of money and want you to give them a couple of days for free; they can't afford a stuntman and would you mind doing your own stunts; it's a very low budget film and do you mind working for much less than your normal fee? It is never, 'I wondered if you'd do me a favour and star in my next big movie?'

With a sinking heart, I said, 'Yes, of course Mr Foreman.'

'Call me Carl.'

'Carl.'

'On Thursday night *The Guns of Navarone*, which I produced, is being shown at the Royal Command Performance and I can't understand half of what Richard Harris says. He plays the Australian bomber pilot and the combination of his Irish brogue and his attempt at an Australian accent has lost all the humour of the part. Would you do me a favour and dub his voice, tomorrow, Tuesday, we're really pushed for time?'

'Yes, of course Mr ... er ... Carl.'

'Thank you Vincent, I really appreciate this.'

Still no mention of whether he liked me in the TV play or not? Heigh ho.

I think that I and every other Australian actor in town had tried to get that part and now I'm dubbing the voice of the actor who got it. It would have been so much simpler if I'd played the part in the first place! But then again, I don't look like Richard Harris, do I?

Next day at the recording studios I met Anthony Quayle, who was doing some post-synching. He was telling me about the making of the film and how Gregory Peck, to retain his lean good looks, was always dieting and often would overdo things to the extent of being so weak from lack of food that the other actors had to get behind him, when climbing ladders, and give him a bit of a shove so he could make it.

Apart from a role in *Carry On Cruising*, the year careerwise was uneventful. Of course, the family and the Old Rectory made up for any disappointment there. It was a magical place, so much so that one didn't really want to work, and then there were the nearby pubs, The Anchor at Stowting and The Gate at Rhodes Minnis, two

of the finest watering holes in East Kent.

The year 1963 started a little better. I was playing 'Digger' in a television production of 'The Hasty Heart' for the BBC in Glasgow. There were rumours that eventually all television drama would be recorded, it wouldn't be too soon for me. These live productions made me very twitchy.

After I did an episode of 'The Planemakers' my agent had a call from the producer of the BBC's 'Compact', a twice weekly series about a magazine, offering me the on-going part of David Rome, showbiz editor.

Doing a live show every week didn't appeal to me very much, but that was overcome by the thought of a regular pay cheque and a certain amount of security. I accepted and made my first appearance with a chimpanzee, who upstaged me all the time *and* got all the close-ups.

What's that old W.C. Fields saying? 'Never work with children or animals.' How right he was.

'Compact' changed my whole way of living. The financial security brought with it a regular absence from the family. I was staying in London from Monday to Saturday, which meant that

Doreen had to cope with three children, her mother and a very large house. Not easy when you don't drive. Of course there was nothing to drive anyway. We only had one car, and I needed it in London.

But cope she did. Splendidly.

Leo McKern, John Meillon, Michael Craig, Donald Houston, Don Chaffey, Lee Montague, Ed Deveraux, Bill Kerr, Les Leston, Vic Friendly, Richard Gregson, Harold and Chris Jamieson were my stable of cricketers who made the pilgrimage each year to test their arm against the Stowting village eleven.

My chaps would be 'lunched' at the Rectory and then shepherded up to the cricket field. Apart from batting, bowling and fielding, my most important job was to restrain them from returning to the Rectory 'to revive their flagging spirits'.

I have such fond memories of those cricket days.

Lord Brabourne, my neighbour, whose pheasants having escaped the guns of Prince Phillip would seek sanctuary in our top half-acre, asked me to be a regular member of his cricket

team to play the Grand Prix drivers in a charity match every two years.

I said I would be delighted.

In one unforgettable match, I was to open the batting with Prince Charles.

While we were padding up, I caught a glimpse of his royal young rump and the unprotected 'crown jewels'. I picked up a 'box' and tossed it to him, saying, 'Charles, I think you should wear one of these.'

A shy 'thank you' and he slipped it into his underpants.

As we walked out to the pitch, I couldn't help thinking that in some small way, I may have helped protect the royal heritage of our future king.

Charles was bowled second ball but the umpire, Stirling Moss, said he wasn't ready, it was a no-ball anyway and apart from that the crowd would lynch him if he gave Charles 'out' so he's still 'in'. Eventually, Charles and I had an opening partnership of thirty-five runs.

He came up to me afterwards, handed me the still warm 'box', shook my hand and said, 'Thank you. It was nice batting with you, Vincent.'

I just wish I'd kept that 'box'. I could have put it next to my 'B' grade tennis cup in the display cabinet, or, when things were a bit tight, sold it: 'Cricket box worn by Prince Charles, never been washed. Offers?'

The regular pay cheque from 'Compact', the uncertainty of the eleven plus school exam and the irregular village bus service were the deciding factors in our decision to send Cathy and Christian to boarding school. Christian to Friars, a prep school at Great Chart, and Cathy to Sibton Park, both within ten miles of the Rectory.

I told myself that I was giving my kids the kind of educational opportunities that I never had, and the right kind of setting for their formative years, the beauty of the English countryside and the Old Rectory.

Now, if you are still interested in this thumb-nail sketch my dear grandchildren, I would like to tell you a little about your parents and their life at the Old Rectory.

It's three-thirty in the afternoon, and by standing and looking out of the living-room windows, I have, now that I've cut the hedge back, a clear view of the village school as it spews its laughing,

squealing, crying pupils out to the doting mums with their Hillmans, Minis, 1100s, Cortinas, and the friendly lady driver of the school bus. Among that squealing mass I have a six-and-a-half year-old son, Jonathan, and it won't be until the last car has gone that he will put in an appearance. Why is it that my son always seems to be the last to walk out the school gate?

Here he comes, no, he's gone again. A wait of another couple of minutes, once more he appears and this time, yes, no, wait a moment, yes, he starts the long trek home, all of 150 yards. I wonder how long it will take him today?

My mind's eye goes into a close-up of what he usually looks like when he comes home from school: the blond hair, ruffled as if it has never seen a brush or comb, his nose running (apparently he's allergic to household dust, and what can you do about that?), the anorak being swung around his head like an Australian stockwhip, dirty knees, socks around his ankles, and to top it all, his fly's undone. My son is no respector of the invention that changed the dressing habits of half the world—the zip fastener.

That's my son, Jonathan.

He's now gone about three yards and it

seems the whole journey has come to a halt because I can only see his rear half, the rest is buried in a hedge. It might be a bird's nest, caterpillar, or it could be nothing. He's in there just having a look. The rest of his body appears and once more, starts off for the Old Rectory.

Hello, he's running. Ah yes, I see the reason, it's a large stone, and he's kicking it along the road, playing football he calls it, the toes of his shoes should be nice and white now, the leather and polish having been left on the stone. One big final kick, and he's decided he doesn't want to be Bobby Charlton any more and the stone is left by the side of the road.

And now comes the daydreaming bit, the anorak trails on the ground, the pace slackens and the little face takes on a faraway look. What does a six and a half year old dream about? Building bridges, maybe being a cowboy, actor, Indian chief, fisherman—I often wonder what I would like him to be when he grows up—a famous surgeon, prime minister, engineer? Ah, who cares, as long as he's happy.

He's disappeared behind the hedge now and in a couple of seconds, or minutes, he will re-appear near the gate and then go through the

kerb drill. His kerb drill consists of swivelling his head from side to side, at the same time rolling his eyes in a circle. He looks like a drunken puppet and that's how he crosses the road.

My son, my son.

'Hello, Jonathan, how was school today?'

'I don't like you. I'm going to leave home, and I didn't eat my lunch.'

Heigh ho. Not one of his best days, it seems.

Exeats were the big days during term time at the Rectory, especially if Cathy and Christian managed by a stroke of luck to have them on the same day.

I'd collect Christian after church at nine-thirty, deliver him to the Old Rectory, have a chat and cup of coffee, and then Doreen or I would head for Folkestone to pick up Cathy. Finally the whole family would be together by about one o'clock.

Cathy liked boarding school. Christian, I think, hated it. He would start looking at his watch at around four o'clock and I'm sure he counted the minutes, dreading the time when he had to leave. His rosy-cheeked face took on a serious expression and he grew quieter and quieter. Cathy, meanwhile, would be raiding the

larder for baked beans, cake, biscuits, anything edible. There was always a midnight feast in the 'dorm' after an exeat.

Six-thirty is zero hour. Cathy, bright and happy, loaded down with provisions, piles into the Mini. Christian, stony-faced, carrying a bag of fruit, they aren't allowed to take anything else, quietly sits in the car.

He never said much on the way back, maybe he didn't have a chance. I kept up an endless stream of chatter, trying to cheer him up. The worst part for him was the final fare-well at the school. He sat in the car until the very last moment, continually looking at his watch, willing, I'm sure, for the bell not to ring.

The bell sounds and in a rush, 'Daddy, I'd better go, you won't forget to write and if you can, will you come and see me. The best time is before prep at about a quarter to four, don't forget.'

A quick kiss and he's gone. Sadly, I won't see him for another four or five weeks.

He was only eight when we sent him to boarding school. I remember I asked him on his first exeat, what his first day was like.

'Alright. All the new boys were put in a special dormitory. There were seven of us. I cried when I went to bed.'

'Did any of the other boys cry?'

'Yes, they all did.'

Seven lonely little boys crying themselves to sleep because their parents, perhaps like me, were doing what they thought was the best thing. Eight is too young to be wrenched away from family life.

Doreen was home when I got back.

'How did he go off?' she asked.

'Oh, just the same. Fighting back the tears. I had a word with Mr Lendrum about how upset he gets. All Mr Lendrum said was, "Don't worry, Mr Ball, most of the boys behave like that to start with. But Christian will be fine. He's made of the right stuff.'"

'You now have ulcers on your ulcers,' said my doctor, Brian Woodward. 'You must think about surgery.'

It was October 1964 and I had been coping with my ulcers for fifteen years, without success. Not really making any serious attempt to cure them. I was still smoking, drinking and eating all

the wrong foods. Now I was getting my come-uppance for all the abuse that I'd heaped upon my body. Surgery. The twice weekly pressure of 'Compact' wasn't helping much either.

A bypass or a partial gastrectomy? I think I got more ulcers trying to make up my mind which to have. When two Harley Street specialists are telling you 'theirs' is best, it's not easy.

Eventually, after about three months, I opted for the partial gastrectomy recommended by Mr Henley, the Harley Street surgeon and husband of well-known actress Elizabeth Sellars. He put me into a rather select hospital, the King Edward VIIth Hospital for Officers near Harley Street and paid for by BUPA (British United Provident Association).

Once again, knowing what they were doing about the rabbit pest in Australia had paid off. I was in a posh hospital, in the Queen Mum's old room with the squeaky bed.

I realised as I looked at a rather ugly twelve inch scar in the shape of a boomerang under my rib cage, that my days of taking my shirt off in front of the cameras were over.

Convalescing at Osborne House in the Isle of Wight, the former holiday home of Queen

Victoria, was really an eye-opener. You could have sworn that the war was still on. Osborne House was conducted like an Officers' Mess and your seating in the dining room was dictated by your rank. You can imagine where I sat, being a lowly Flying Officer.

Doreen was coming over to see me and the arrival of the ferry from Southhampton coincided with dinnertime on a Friday night. And would you believe it, I had to go up to the main table and say, 'Excuse me, sir,' to an ex-admiral, 'my wife is arriving by ferry, sir. Permission to leave the mess, sir?'

'Yes, righto. Carry on. What's your name?'

'Ball, sir.'

'Yes, carry on Ball.'

The year is 1965! And we are all civilians!

I didn't do too well at Osborne House. When asked what I would like to do for occupational therapy, I said, I would like to paint. On arrival next morning to start my therapy, I found an easel, several canvases, a palette, brushes and many tubes of paint, waiting to be mixed.

'No, when I said I would like to paint, I meant walls, doors, chairs, things like that,' I

explained. I really went down in their estimation. Probably they thought that being an actor, I was artistic.

So that's what I did at Osborne House. If it didn't move I painted it.

Back to reality and after a six weeks' absence, back to 'Compact'. The powers that be at the BBC, however, in their wisdom decided to cut the programme. It wasn't the ratings, which were still high, but I think they felt that 'Compact', a successful soapy, was the wrong image for the BBC. Goodbye security.

We were all in need of a break by the time 'Compact' finished in July 1965, so I loaded the family into the station wagon and set off for Bill Kerr's villa in the hills behind St Pedro el Cantara, Spain, where we would be joined by our dear friend, the children's favourite adopted aunt, Carmen Silvera, now one of the stars of ''Allo 'Allo'. Our neighbour would be Hattie Jaques and the red wine would be ninepence a litre. All the makings of a splendid holiday.

Then it was back to being a jobbing actor and the years 1966 to 1970 had much of a sameness—theatre tours, films, episodes in the

various television series, regular stints in 'Crossroads' and, of course, the *resting* periods.

The highlights were doing a Lonsdale comedy *Aren't We All* at the Theatre Royal, Windsor, and transferring to the Savoy Theatre in the West End. Unfortunately it coincided with a heat wave and Wimbledon—we lasted eight weeks. A tour of *The Flipside* with Neil McCallum; working with Richard Burton and Clint Eastwood in *Where Eagles Dare*; getting a call from Richard Attenborough to play the 'Australian' in *Oh! What a Lovely War*; and filming with Robert Goulert and a couple of other actors—the four of us wiping out half the German Army in the streets of Munich, watched by a crowd of stony-faced middle-aged spectators who were, no doubt, remembering the war.

Many people outside the business think that making a movie is all glamour, but I can assure you it has its downside.

The routine when filming in the studio was for the actors to do a 'walk through' for the moves and positions of the scene about to be shot, then the lighting people take over and the set is 'lit'. The time varies, of course, and while this is happening the actors either go back to

their dressing rooms or sit in the chairs provided for them on the set. If you're important enough you get one with your name on it! This is the boring part of filming—the waiting and the hanging about.

Where Eagles Dare was an exception to the rule. Richard Burton would give the signal and an entourage of actors would form and, like the Pied Piper of Hamelin, he would lead us off to his dressing room where drinks would be dispensed by his personal make-up man and Richard would hold court, regaling us with amusing stories of Wales, Rugby and theatre. He talked of the theatre with affection but always in the past tense and one got the feeling of regret, that he had forsaken his first love—the stage— for Hollywood. He hardly ever mentioned films and if he did, they were the butt of some joke that would have his captive audience falling about with laughter.

Yeah, *Where Eagles Dare* was different.

The situation had arisen where I was spending all my time away from the Rectory, mostly touring, to earn enough money to keep the place going, pay the school fees and keep the tax man happy. It

wasn't much fun for Doreen, who rattled around the house with only her mother and Jonathan for company. Being a leading light in the Lyminge Dramatic Society was a welcome diversion.

Often the word 'amateur' implies that something is mediocre. This was not the case with the Lyminge Dramatic Society, whose standard of production and performance were on a par and sometimes better than a lot of 'professional' companies I've been associated with. They were a friendly, fun-loving group that enhanced our years in the Elham Valley. Those friendships still remain to this day.

We sold the Old Rectory in 1970 and moved to Orchard End, Ottinge, a small picture-postcard, tile-hung Kent cottage with roses around the door. Cathy and Christian became day pupils and Doreen's mum went to a nursing home in Hythe.

We found it difficult to recover from selling the Old Rectory and on top of that my career now was continually taking me away from home. I was going from one theatre tour to another. It was an unsettling period. My prolonged absences were stretching our family relationship to breaking point.

It was at this time that I cheated on Doreen.

I was middle-aged. I know that's no excuse. I was flattered by the attentions of an attractive young woman, and the relationship produced a daughter called Emily.

Doreen was deeply hurt. It would take a long time to heal the wound and maybe be forgiven, if I was ever given the opportunity to try.

'I have no intention of divorcing you, leaving home or asking you to go,' she said when I broached the subject. 'If you want to, we could try and pick up the threads of our marriage, think of the children, keep our family together and get on with our lives. What do you say?'

'Yes, I would like that,' I said, grateful to be given the chance to repair the damage I had caused.

'You'll give a performance to mixed audiences in each city,' my agent said. I believed him.

'Open in Cape Town, play Jo'burg, Durban and Port Elizabeth. Rehearsals in Jo'burg. You'll be away three months.'

John Gregson and I were to go from London; Joan Fontaine and a New York actor

from America. We would pick up the other member of the cast in Jo'burg. The play was *Dial M for Murder*.

Generally the play opens with Joan's and my character sitting on a sofa having a conversation. Not for Joan. She insisted that she make an 'entrance'. Fair enough, I suppose. After all, she was the big star.

So now the play opens with me on the sofa, speaking all my lines to Joan who is off-stage, supposedly in the garden. After this one-sided conversation, she would enter upstage centre, through the french windows, sweep down centre stage to a round of applause. As I said, fair enough.

Opening night, she swept down stage to a round of applause and said ... nothing. Her lips moved and that's about all. I repeated my line, and the same thing happened again. I knew that I hadn't gone deaf because I could hear my own voice and the rustling of the audience.

Joan had lost her voice.

I tried to give one of my 'cool' looks as I watched the curtain slowly come down.

After four days Joan got her voice back. But we never did play to mixed audiences.

Segregated was suggested, but the black Africans said, 'No. Mixed or nothing.'

The South African actor in the cast was Anthony Wheeler, a fine human being, now living in Australia and one of my best mates.

It's wintertime, I'm in the middle of the Pyrenees, the snow is piled about twelve feet high on either side of a single-track roadway, I'm driving a Morris 1100, full of pushchair sand-tracks, and all I've got in case of an emergency is a bottle of whisky.

How did I get into that situation?

I got there because an actor mate, Neil McCallum, had asked me to invest one hundred pounds in a business venture.

'Renting pushchairs to tourists on the Costa Brava and Majorca.'

I agreed to be an investor. Then about five minutes later, he rings back and says, 'How would you like to be a director?'

'What would I have to do?'

'Come with me to Barcelona, form a company, buy a few hundred pushchairs, ship them over to Majorca, where my niece, a travel courier for Horizon Tours, will organise the

rentals through all the other couriers from tour companies. They will work on a commission basis. Most mums with small children have to either carry them or buy a pushchair and then leave it behind when they return to the UK, because they're not allowed to take them on the aircraft. And I have this new invention "sand-tracks" which enable the pushchairs to be pushed over the sand without bogging down. There are 3000 hotels in Majorca. We'll do a test run there. The British Board of Trade said that it was the best original idea they've heard of in ten years. What do you say?'

'Ah . . . Yes.'

Two days later, Neil informed me that he'd been offered a part in a film being shot on the US Aircraft Carrier *Forrestall* in the Mediterranean, finishing up at Barcelona and it clashed with our proposed trip.

'I need the money. I'll have to do the film,' he said.

I can still hear myself saying it, 'You go ahead. I'll go down to Barcelona and form the company and organise the pushchairs. Just make sure that your niece is there to interpret for me. I'll see you in Barcelona.'

I appeared out of a snowstorm at the Spanish border, where the guards, after indicating that I was crazy to have driven over the mountains, impounded the car until they could figure out what the sand-tracks were for.

Even though I had all the correct import papers, it was quite difficult to explain to them how the sand-tracks worked. Especially when I didn't speak Spanish, they didn't speak English and I didn't have a pushchair to demonstrate with.

They eventually gave up and waved me on my way.

In Barcelona, with the help of Neil's niece, I did all the things I was supposed to do and waited for Neil.

Two days before he was due to arrive, the British Consul received two cables from our agents saying that they had accepted parts in a prestigious play for the BBC and would we come back right away. Rehearsals would start the following Monday. It was now Thursday.

Neil arrived on the Saturday and I drove us from Barcelona to Calais without sleep, just catching the cross-Channel ferry Sunday morning.

We did the play and set off for Spain once more.

In Majorca it took us seven days to find Neil's niece. She was in hospital having a nervous breakdown after a row with her boy-friend. The last things she wanted to talk about were babies and pushchairs.

So there we were, with a warehouse full of pushchairs, unable to speak the language and no couriers to help us out.

We approached several hotels and tried to come to some arrangement. They thought it was a *splendid* idea and immediately went out and bought their own pushchairs.

It took us ten weeks to go broke. But broke we went, and that's why I'm still a jobbing actor and not a tycoon on the Spanish Riviera. Now you'll understand, my dear grandchildren, why you didn't receive a legacy from your grandpa.

fourteen

COMING HOME

'WHY DON'T WE GO back to Australia?' Doreen said. 'And maybe, just maybe, we might be able to live as a family. You're never here—always touring or whatever. The family never see you. Anyway, I think the change would do us the world of good. It's not the same here any more, not since we sold the Rectory.'

Cathy, a student at the Guildhall School of Music and Drama, stayed behind and the rest of us headed back to the land of my birth.

In Australia I wasn't exactly the new boy on the block, more your new middle-aged boy on the block and after the initial euphoria of my reunion with the family and mates and being looked after by June Cann Management, the work rolled in.

Eric Tayler gave me the lead in a play for ABC Television; Michael Craig directed me in

the play *Move over Mrs Markham*; Neil Mc-Callum, now a producer with the BBC, came out to produce the 'Ben Hall' series, and Don Chaffey was the director. All mates. How could I go wrong?

I played a character called Sergeant Garland in all the episodes of 'Ben Hall'. It was the nearest I ever came to realising my dream. I was the leader of the troopers, a sort of deputy sheriff. I rode a horse, carried a six-gun and was always shouting, very loudly, '*Follow me*' as we chased the baddies.

After six months of film shoot-outs, bail-ups, cock-ups and blacktrackers, we finally gave Ben Hall, the notorious bushranger, his comeuppance.

From that straight into another period series about the gold rush days. It was aptly called 'Rush'. This time I was the boss: the superintendent. Still chasing the baddies, riding a big white horse, carrying a six-gun and still shouting, '*Follow me*'. In America, I would have been the marshall.

The family had settled in pretty well to their new life in Australia. The boys were in good schools and Doreen was in the process of

forming her own theatre company, the Players Theatre Company. My career had moved into second gear. I worked pretty regularly but I wasn't 'new' any more and I was available.

Neil McCallum, after finishing the final editing on 'Ben Hall', returned to England. Within six weeks he was dead. His children found him on the kitchen floor early one morning. He had died from a brain haemorrhage. Dear Neil. He'd been a good friend.

Returning home after another 'Cop Shop' in Melbourne, I was greeted by a grave-faced Doreen, who told me that Christian had terminal cancer. I didn't take it in at first. It seemed only yesterday that we had attended his passing out parade at Kapooka Army Training Camp. How could this tall, lean, bronzed young soldier of nineteen suddenly have terminal cancer?

He'd always wanted to be a soldier. Even as a little boy he was obsessed with uniforms and probably had one of the finest collections of hand-painted toy soldiers in the county of Kent.

When, in Australia, he told me that he was going to join the Army, I begged him to gain the right qualifications and join as a trainee officer.

'I've been through the ranks and I know,' I told him. But he couldn't wait, he joined anyway.

Christian sat on the edge of his bed at Ingleburn Army Hospital and calmly and quietly asked the question, 'Am I going to die?'

Without the slightest hesitation his mother replied, 'Of course you are not going to die, darling.'

It was the way she said it. She sort of ... spelt it out, quietly and firmly, with an intense conviction that did not brook arguments or doubts.

He was taken to the Prince of Wales Hospital, where they pumped sixteen different kinds of drugs into him for twenty-four hours a day. After four weeks of chemotherapy we brought him home. His doctor had told us that Christian had about six weeks to live.

He stood in the hallway of our home at Wollstonecraft and held out his hands to both of us saying, 'Mum, Dad, don't treat me as an invalid.'

We joined hands, as his mother said, 'We won't. We'll all think positively.'

Christian is now thirty-nine. He, with the help of his dedicated doctors, licked that cancer.

I take my hat off to my son. I'd like to think that I could handle something like that as well as he did. As his schoolmaster said when he was eight years old, 'Don't worry about Christian, Mr Ball. He's made of the right stuff.'

'Twenty-four hours in an eight-day week would not fit my needs', were the words of Mr Jaggers, a character I once played in *Great Expectations*, and they just about summed up my association with Doreen's Players Theatre Company.

I whinged a lot, but as one of its four directors, barman, cleaner, jack of all trades, it was one of the most satisfying periods in my career as an actor.

The advantages of being a boss is, of course, that you have the choice of parts. Well, there's not much point in having a theatre company if you don't indulge yourself a bit, is there? It makes up for all the late hours, lack of money, the building of sets and cleaning the auditorium before going on stage at night to play Henry in *The Lion in Winter*. A process that never changed in all the other plays I did with that company.

I just wish there were no such things as first

nights. If only one could open on the second night. How you work that I don't know, but I've never been able to overcome my first-night nerves. I thought that as the years went by and I became more experienced, things would get better. No such luck, they became worse if anything. I dunno what it is. Is it the fear of 'drying', making a fool of myself, worried about the critics out front or what? Is it wanting to be liked, wanting to be good? Maybe it's a bit of everything. Then why do it, you may well ask. It's simple ... I love it.

Doreen never stopped. She directed, acted, made costumes, applied for grants and with the help of directors Graham Corry and Graham Dixon, surrounded herself with a lot of 'company minded' actors, who could turn their hands to almost anything and were as enthusiastic as she was.

We were four years at the Bondi Pavilion Theatre, from 1979 to 1982, and during that time I did very little television, but parts in the films *Breaker Morant* and *Phar Lap* helped to keep the wolf from actually coming through the door.

Artistically the Players Theatre Company

was a great success. We had splendid support from the neighbouring suburbs and a small grant from the Premier's Department. The Australia Council offered to come to the party, if the Waverley Council would match them dollar-for-dollar.

The Waverley Council refused.

We asked them for a three-year lease, so that we could plan our productions ahead and start a subscription programme. Again Waverley Council refused.

We'd had enough. We told them to 'stick it', and once again the Bondi Pavilion Theatre went into a decline. A pity. We had built up a loyal following, which was increasing each year. People of the theatre should run theatres and aldermen should stick to running local councils.

Cathy, our lovely daughter, who had come out from England while we were running the Bondi Pavilion Theatre, was a tower of strength and her experience in the London theatres was invaluable. Our little girl was now a bubbly, talented, generous, warm-hearted human being in her early twenties.

I suppose it was inevitable that she would marry an actor and she did, English actor Paul

Mason, and they presented us with grandson Nicholas. Paul and I had worked together on 'Rush'.

Christian was at Mitchell College, Bathurst. Jonathan went to Sydney University, got himself an aeronautical engineering degree and joined the Navy! All the children had flown the coop, so Doreen and I moved to Balmoral Beach on beautiful Sydney Harbour. We now run the cheapest seaside laundry, motel, always open cafe in town, and we wouldn't have it any other way.

It was the 1988 Rugby League Grand Final. Canterbury-Bankstown were playing Balmain and the whole Ball family, Brian, Moya, Noni, Clete, Joe, Phil and myself were squashed into Mum's room at the Stella Maris Nursing Home at Cronulla, willing Canterbury to win because Mum had said 'they were a good Catholic team'!

We were gathered there because Mum, whose health had been deteriorating over the past twenty-four hours, had expressed the wish that all her children watch the match with her. So there we were, taking it in turns to hold her hands as we watched the Rugby League Grand

Final. Just before half-time Mum slipped into a deep coma but we continued to watch the TV, finding it difficult to appreciate what was happening on the screen, only thinking of Mum.

I'm sure we all felt the same. How do you say thank you for all the years of uncomplaining struggle and sacrifice that she had gone through for all of us. My big brother Brian, a master builder. Moya, a happy housewife. Noni, my little sister Noni, who I was so worried about during the war because of her wish to be a Sister of Mercy teaching nun. She got her wish, taught for many years in various schools around Sydney and then in her fifties went to a drama school, became a qualified elocutionist and now runs a drama school at Parramatta Convent. Cletus, my brother Clete. Ex-tumbler, acrobat, adagio dancer and currently a clown. He travelled the world with the Dior Dancers and his own act, the Bal-Caron Trio; played the Palladium four or five times; the Lido in Paris; Las Vegas; Miami; and did two Royal Command performances.

Three of us virtually in show business—was one of our Irish ancestors a strolling player? Where did we get this urge to perform in public?

Joe, a banker and father of six. Philomena, who followed sister Noni into the convent only to be forced to leave because of back problems. She couldn't handle all that kneeling. Now she is a happy housewife and mother of three.

Yeah, you did a pretty good job Bridget Rose. A pretty good job ...

Brian patted Mum's hand: 'Bridget Rose, Canterbury-Bankstown has won twenty-four to twelve.'

Noni and I would stay with Mum during the night and let the rest of the family know if anything happened.

It was about ten o'clock. There were two nuns, Noni and myself in the room. I was standing holding Mum's hand watching the faint pulse in her neck as she gently slipped away, without any stress or discomfort, her face suddenly smooth as if the cares of the world had been lifted from her. This dear lady, my ninety-year-old mum was gently dying. I'm sure she planned it that way. Without fuss or bother, surrounded by people who loved her.

My thoughts weren't making much sense, they were jumping from one thing to another. It was like a kaleidoscope, trying to compress a

lifetime in those few short minutes. I kept thinking of her gentleness, her caring and the love she
shared equally among us, no favourites, or if
there were she didn't let us know.

And my guilt: wishing I had written more
often, remembered more birthdays and Mother's
Days in the twenty-five years I was in England;
hoping she would not come out of the coma and
linger on for a few more days. My mum was just
worn out and her body had said 'enough'.

'She's gone Vince,' one of the nuns said.

I still held her hand. I was sure I could feel her
pulse and she might just be able to feel my hand.

'She's gone Vince.'

I leaned down and kissed her. 'Goodbye
Bridget Rose.'

Yeah, I'll back my mum against anybody's.

My grateful thanks to those caring, loving
sisters, Clare Coyle and Mary de Monfort, who with
all the staff of Stella Maris made my mum's stay and
going so comfortable and painless. God bless.

It was about seven am at Smokey Dawson's in
Terrey Hills. I was on location for the mini-series
'Bangkok Hilton' and Denholm Elliot arrived
looking very much the worse for wear—a large

hangover I should say. After a subdued 'Good-morning', he sat down beside me and stared off into the bush for at least a full five minutes. Then he turned to me and said, in his beautifully modulated English voice: 'You do a very good Chardonnay here,' and stared off into the bush again.

I suppose this book is about memories. When you look back maybe it *is* through rose-coloured glasses, but you try to hang onto times, places and people that gave you pleasure, and this wouldn't be complete without a salute to all those mates I started out with in the late 1940s and early '50s.

We roamed the parties of London, living it up and battling for recognition as actors. They were exciting times. To those mates who have departed to 'the big Rep in the sky,' I 'tip me lid' to you: Stanley Baker, Don Chaffey, Peter Finch, Nigel Green, Donald Houston, Harold Jamieson, John Meillon, Neil McCallum and Robert Shaw. I treasure those memories we shared together. If Jonesy, my old wartime mate, should come looking for a party, let him in, he's one of us.

And a special thanks to Bill Kerr, for forty hilarious years of 'can I come around for a cup of tea and fifteen minutes of worry?'

That's just about it, my grandchildren. I haven't given you long lists of the television programmes, films and plays that I've done. They wouldn't mean much to you anyway. As your grandma said, it's just a thumbnail sketch!

Aw, but what the hell. I *did* work and maybe I shouldn't hide my light under a bushel. Well, that's what my agent was always telling me. So to all you insomniacs, night owls and nightwatchmen who, in the early hours of the morning, turn to the telly for a bit of light relief, you may, you just may, catch one of my old movies from the list I am now going to leave with you ... and jolly good luck.

1949 *The Blue Lagoon*
      Warning to Wantons
      The Interrupted Journey
      Stop Press Girl
1950 *Come Dance With Me*
1951 *Talk of a Million*
      London Entertains
      Encore
1953 *The Drayton Case*
1954 *The Dark Stairway*
      Dangerous Voyage

Devil's Harbour
Stolen Time
The Black Rider
1955 John and Julie
The Blue Peter
The Big Fish
1956 The Baby and the Battleship
A Town Like Alice
Secret of the Forest
1957 Face in the Night
Robbery Under Arms
1958 Blood of the Vampire
Sea of Sand
1959 Danger Within
Summer of the Seventeenth Doll
1960 Dentist in the Chair
Identity Unknown
Feet of Clay
Dead Lucky
1961 Nearly A Nasty Accident
Very Important Person
Highway to Battle
The Middle Course
A Matter of WHO
1962 Carry on Cruising
1963 Echo of Diana

   Mouse on the Moon
1967 *Follow That Camel*
1968 *Where Eagles Dare*
1969 *Oh! What a Lovely War*
1971 *Not Tonight Darling*
1972 *Clinic Xclusive*
1976 *Death Cheaters*
1978 *The Irishman*
1979 *Alison's Birthday*
1980 *Breaker Morant*
1981 *Deadline*
1982 *The Southern Cross/The Highest Honour*
1983 *Phar Lap*
1985 *Flight into Hell*
1986 *Double Sculls*
1987 *The Year My Voice Broke*
1990 *Turtle Beach*
1991 *Frauds*
1993 *Sirens*
1993 *Muriel's Wedding*

Still awake?

I should, at this stage, leave you with some *words of wisdom*, some *sound advice*. I can't think of anything, except maybe, Never lose your sense of humour.

I enjoyed trying to make my living as an actor. I have regrets, because I once had a dream.

I never did walk down Main Street at noon, my hand hovering near my six-guns.

Never did say 'Go for yer gun'.

Never rode with a posse.

Never faced down an angry crowd as sheriff of a Wild West town, and never became known as the 'fastest gun in the West' or even gave a lazy crooked smile.

Never got the girl and rode off into the sunset.

Never had that elusive 'something' to separate me from the crowd and make me a star.

There are other regrets too. Things I would like to change. I never played it *all* according to the rules, and so I hurt people in the process.

I regret that I cheated and destroyed the trust your grandma placed in me but I cannot deny that I am proud to be the father of Emily, an attractive, talented, Oxford University honours graduate, for whose achievements I can take no credit. Her mother deserves all that.

She made all the sacrifices and as a single mum the going was pretty tough.

Your grandma invited Emily to stay with us in 1990. Now let's face it, there aren't many

wives who would invite the offspring of a wayward husband's extra-marital relationship into her home for a holiday, is there?

For the six months she stayed with us at Balmoral, your parents, all my brothers, sisters, nephews, nieces and friends made her most welcome and treated her as one of the family. For that I thank them and am eternally grateful for their understanding.

I suppose you could call me the black sheep of the family; I do believe some other families have them as well! But then again I was lucky enough to have a generous and forgiving wife with a sense of humour who, for forty-six years, when asked annually what she was giving me for Christmas, would always come up with her stock reply of, 'I'm letting him stay another year.'

I don't think I would match up to my screen heroes, Buck Jones, Tom Mix and Tim McCoy.

All in all, it's been a pretty good life and it's not over yet; but when it is and I've joined my mates in 'the big Rep in the sky', no doubt you will simply sum me up in five words . . .

'My grandpa was an actor'.

INDEX

Ball, Vincent *(cont'd.)*
school sports, 96–8,
103; same class as
Brian, 97; gets
Intermediate
Certificate, 104;
breaks arm, 106;
early jobs, 107–9;
first holiday, 110;
first sexual
experience, 115–19,
125–6; French letters,
120–2; confesses
intercourse, 127–9; in
accountancy, 132;
joins RAAF, 133;
posted to Canada,
135; Wireless Air
Gunner, 135;
hitchhikes to
Hollywood, 141–6,
150–1; and to
Calgary, 153–9;
AWL, 159–60;
gunnery school, 162;
operational training,
163–4; posted to
Cornwall, 165; Syd's
death, 166–9; caught
with his pants down,
173; applies for
commission, 175–9,
181; receives
commission, 183–4;
goes to Dublin,
186–9; questions
Catholic faith, 191–2,
194–6; serves Mass,
193–7; U-boat hunt,
203–5; radar
instructor, 207;
Australian troops
grounded, 208; leaves
England, 210; reasons
for enlisting, 212;
arrives home, 215–16;
reveals acting
ambition, 220; acting
dream, 221–3;
elocution lessons,
224–9; seeing Doreen,
233; broken dagger,

373

Burton, Richard, 342, 343

Caine, Michael, 311
Caldwell, Ken
  'Professor', 168, 179, 183, 210
Callan Park, 89–94
Campion, Gerry, 298
Carey, Brother, 80, 81, 84, 91
Carrington, Ethel, 275
Carry on Cruising (film), 329, 364
Carshalton, Surrey, 285
Carstairs, John Paddy, 277
Chaffey, Don: directs VB, 311; VB's friend, 322; Christmas 1961, 327; VB's cricket XI, 331; directs *Ben Hall*, 352; VB remembers, 362
Chaffey, Edna, 322
Charles, Prince, 332

Chiari, Walter, 320
Christian Brothers College, Burwood, 105
Christian Brothers College, Rozelle, 74, 78
Clinic Xclusive (film), 365
Colbert, Claudette, 153
Collins, Joan, 270
Come Dance With Me (film), 363
Commonwealth Rhodes Trust fund, 264
Compact (TV series), 330, 341
Confiteor, Mother, 10
Cop Shop (TV series), 353
Corry, Graham, 356
Cowan, Theo, 294
Coyle, Sister Clare, 361
Craig, Jannette, 318
Craig, Michael, 309, 310, 326, 331, 351

Haifa, 240

Halifax Building Society, 285, 323

Hallet, Neil, 250

Harben Road, Swiss Cottage, 291

Harris, Richard, 328

Harrop, Doreen (*see* Ball, Doreen)

Harrop, Mr (Doreen's father), 266, 287

Harrop, Mrs (Doreen's mother), 266, 287, 323, 344

Hasty Heart, The (TV series), 330

Henley, Mr (surgeon), 339

Henry IV (play), 260

Henry V (play), 271

Herbert, Percy, 309

Highest Honour, The (film), 323

Highway to Battle (film), 364

Hill, Jacqueline, 280

Hill, Syd (Siddy): finds Robbo, 139; agrees to hitchhike, 140–1, 143; loses money belt, 144; finds money in pamphlet, 149; hitchhikes to Calgary, 153–9; AWL, 159–60; posted to Cornwall, 165; missing in action, 166; toasted, 210

Hippolytus (play), 233

Hollywood, 151–3

Hollywood Canteen, 151–2

Houston, Donald: uses VB as double, 249; budding actor, 280; films with VB, 311; Christmas 1961, 326; VB's cricket XI, 331; VB remembers, 362

'Hovel, The', Seymour Place, 260

Howard, Trevor, 318

379

Hurt, John, 324
Hutton, Betty, 152

Ideal Home, 281
Identity Unknown
  (film), 364
Interrupted Journey,
  The (film), 363
Irishman, The (film),
  365
J. Arthur Rank Films,
  294, 295

James, Lyn, 324
James, Syd, 278
Jamieson, Chris, 331
Jamieson, Harold
  (Jamie): suggests VB
  go to RADA, 259–60;
  coaches VB, 261–2;
  gets VB a flat, 267;
  budding actor, 280;
  script writer, 296;
  buys VB's tithe barn,
  324; VB's cricket XI,
331; VB remembers,
  362
Janni, Joe, 290–1,
  297–8, 299
Janni, Mrs, 290
Jaques, Hattie, 341
John and Julie (film),
  364
Jones, Owen (Jonesy):
  gets drunk with VB,
  135; delegates VB,
  137; fails morse code
  exam, 138; separated
  from VB, 140; keeps
  in touch, 198–203;
  boozing, 199–203;
  enlisted, 212; returns
  home, 219; VB
  remembers, 362
June Cann Management,
  351
'Junior Television',
  295–6, 298, 303–9
Jurado, Katy, 318

Kangaroo Paddock, 312

Kelly, Ginger, 88, 90–1, 92, 94, 99

Kerr, Bill, 312, 331, 341, 362

Kilensky, Lee, 144

Kit, Aunty, 110–13, 131

Lachine, Quebec, 163

Ladd, Alan, 152

Lansbury, Angela, 318

Launder, Frank, 238

Lee, Bernard, 311

Lee, Jack, 290, 292, 293, 297

Lendrum, Mr, 338

Leslie, Joan, 151, 153

Leston, Les, 331

Lethbridge, 162

Leuchars, Scotland, 178

Lewis, Ronald, 288

Liberace, 296

Light of Heart (play), 260

Lion in Winter, The (play), 355

London Entertains (film), 363

London Palladium, 296

Lundigan, William, 288

Lyminge Dramatic Society, 344

Lynch, Paddy, 186

Lyons, Joe, 287

Lyons Cadby Hall, 281

McAnally, Ray, 309

McCallum, Neil, 342, 347–50, 352, 353, 362

McCauley, Mr, 4–5, 52

McDermott, Father, 13, 26–8

McDermott, Jacky, 22

McGoohan, Pat, 294

McIlwraith's grocery store, 94

McKenna, Virginia, 288, 290, 293

McKern, Leo, 313, 331

McMaster, Mr, 109

Turtle Beach (film), 365
Tuttle, Father: Mission
   Week, 9; teases Sister
   Ellis, 10; behaviour in
   Mass, 13–14; bell
   tolling, 18; confession,
   26, 35; test catechism,
   48; John's funeral,
   50–1
Twickenham Studios,
   300

United Services
   Organisation, 154,
   155

Van Thal, Denis, 249,
   250
Very Important Person
   (film), 364

WAAFs, 210–11
Warner, Jack, 278
Warning to Wantons
   (film), 363

Warren, Ken J., 312
Waverley Council, 357
Wee Waa, 58
Wheeler, Anthony, 347
Where Eagles Dare
   (film), 342, 343, 365
White, Chalky, 137
Whitehall Academy of
   Dramatic Art, 220,
   221, 224, 235, 237
Wild, Mrs, 4, 65
Wilding, Michael, 311
Winfield, Joan, 152
'WITS' club, 312
Wolfit, Sir Donald, 300
Wollstonecraft, 354
Woodward, Brian, 338

*Year My Voice Broke,
   The* (film), 365
YMCA, Los Angeles,
   143, 150
YMCA, Portland, 157
Young, Loretta, 152